ADVANCE

"Amy argues for the empathy and compassion one might show to a family member or friend to be brought into the business arena; apart from this being the right thing to do, it also helps people engage with each other in such a manner that it is good for profits too. Laced with anecdotes and thorough research, this easily readable book will challenge people to rethink how they understand employees."

KRISS AKABUSI, MBE, Olympian,
Professional Speaker and Transitions Coach

"This is a book for all those CEOs who are grappling with how to build organizations that enhance employees' lives; learn to improve employee, team and organization performance and establish a legacy that helps to create a better world. Compassion is central to all."

GEOFF MCDONALD, Former Vice President, Unilever and Global Mental Health Campaigner and Consultant

"A vital read for any leader wanting to succeed in business today. Importantly, it taps into the very nature of how to understand and connect with employees."

PETE MARKEY, Chief Marketing Officer, TSB

Published by
LID Publishing Limited
The Record Hall, Studio 204,
16-16a Baldwins Gardens,
London EC1N 7RJ, UK

info@lidpublishing.com
www.lidpublishing.com

A member of:

BPR
Business Publishers Roundtable
www.businesspublishersroundtable.com

Printed by TJ International Ltd, Padstow, Cornwall
ISBN: 978-1-912555-28-4

Cover and page design: Matthew Renaudin

THE
HUMAN
MOMENT

AMY BRADLEY

THE POSITIVE POWER OF COMPASSION IN THE WORKPLACE

MADRID | MEXICO CITY | LONDON
NEW YORK | BUENOS AIRES
BOGOTA | SHANGHAI | NEW DELHI

CONTENTS

For Flo and Anne

PREFACE

I have been working with individuals and organizations for many years and every time I talk about the topics covered in this book, it strikes a chord. When I present at conferences about my belief that our workplaces are becoming increasingly transactional, audiences nod vigorously. I describe my observation of 'busyness' in organizations, which means people are so preoccupied with their own tasks and 'to do' lists that their capacity to notice and care for themselves, let alone their colleague down the corridor, is diminished. I witness how our reliance on technology to communicate means that our opportunities to connect and care for one another at a basic human level are decreasing.

I have been asked on countless occasions to give advice to leaders and managers who struggle to know how to deal with a direct report who is going through a difficult life experience. When I work with teams and groups, I can see how superficially they know their colleagues when it comes to their life journeys and the experiences that have shaped them. I see time and again that when we have the courage to disclose our struggles to our colleagues, our work relationships can profoundly deepen. So, I have embarked on a decade-long crusade with employers to help them realize the power of compassion at work.

As we move into a world driven by artificial intelligence and automation, this book aims to help us realize the power of human-to-human connections. Consequently, *The Human Moment* is a practical and accessible guide to help leaders, managers, working professionals and the HR community to embed compassion in their organizations as a foundation for a healthier, happier, more engaged and higher-performing workplace.

1

INTRODUCTION

Whether we are aged 18 or 80, each of us will have experienced defining moments in our life journeys. These 'watershed' events often shape us and I am reminded of the power of difficult life experiences each time I talk about my own. I do not recount my story very often these days. My life has moved on and is markedly different from how it was then. I'm now married. I have a wonderful husband. I have a daughter and three stepchildren. My life is rich and fulfilled. But when people ask how I became interested in compassion at work, I tell them about a period of traumatic and intense suffering, when I experienced compassion first-hand. I also recount some of the human moments I have shared since then that have profoundly strengthened my relationships both at home and at work. In my early thirties and six months pregnant with my daughter, my partner at the time was killed in a freak accident. In the months that followed, I sleep-walked through a fog of grief. I barely functioned. I existed from day to day, discombobulated as I simultaneously struggled to come to terms with bereavement and motherhood. I experienced many gestures of compassion at that time. One such human moment is encapsulated in a letter written by my then manager:

19 September 2006

Dear Amy,

I am writing to express my heartfelt sorrow at your tragic loss. You have been in my thoughts and prayers since the moment I heard of Andy's death. There is little anyone can say or do to comfort you in these darkest hours, but I want you to know that I feel deeply for what you must be going through and share your suffering. I can only hope that in the midst of all the pain and anxiety, your customary courage and resolve will also come through. All your friends – and you have many – and colleagues have been very saddened by this tragedy, and they have all been asking after you. This is testimony to the widespread affection everyone here has for you. I know I am speaking on behalf of everybody when I say that we are here for you, in sympathy and support. We miss you acutely, but we obviously do not want you to be burdened by thoughts of work. You are welcome to return at a time and in a manner of your choice, after your maternity leave. Meanwhile, I know you are with your family, but if you'd like someone else to talk with, or if there are any specific matters you'd like any assistance with, or even just any errands you'd like me to run, please just call.

No one could have predicted that it would be a tragedy of my own that would lead me into my current scholarship and practice. However, in the 13 years that have passed since this sudden bereavement, my research on the topic of personal trauma and professional growth has gained me a doctorate[1] and I have established an educational practice educational practice working with individuals and organizations to better support suffering in the workplace. Furthermore, in my executive education work, I notice that companies are increasingly interested in what it takes to build a more 'human' workplace, where concern for individual wellbeing and engagement is firmly at its heart, and that in a drive to build fairer, more inclusive and more sustainable business models, there is a growing number of calls for compassion to be at the heart of social change.[2]

This book focuses most closely on experiences of bereavement or critical illness (such as cancer); however, that is not to say that experiencing compassion in the face of other types of suffering, such as disability, mental health challenges, redundancy or family breakdown, is not equally relevant. This book contains data from research that has been conducted with working professionals over a ten-year period. I am immensely grateful to each of these individuals who have given me their time and their trust. Were it not for their courage to share their stories, this book would not have been possible. I am mindful that for some of these people, it was the first time they had spoken out loud about their suffering, so I was the first person to hear their stories. I take that responsibility seriously and hope that sharing parts of their stories in this book will help organizations to learn to better support suffering in the workplace. I am also hugely thankful to the companies featured in this book, which features three case studies: Yodel, Outpost VFX and The Interior Design Partnership. It was following a call on LinkedIn that I was able to find and feature this small set of consciously compassionate companies, since the sad reality is that these kinds of organization are few and far between.

In my education, research and coaching work, I have been asked by managers, HR professionals and individuals many times for a practical guide to use when grappling with how to best support suffering at work. People often struggle to know what to say or do to best support their colleagues. Good intentions can be misinterpreted or seen as misguided, simply because of a lack of knowledge of the individual who is suffering, or a lack of experience in this regard. Consequently, this book is aimed at those people who want to develop more 'human' ways of leading or managing. It is also suitable for HR professionals and executive coaches who are looking to support individuals in the wake of suffering. Additionally, employees working alongside colleagues who are facing a difficult episode in their lives may find this book useful. Finally, individuals themselves who are grappling with the challenges of work in the face of suffering may find this book to be a helpful companion.

This book is structured as follows. In the next chapter, a spotlight is thrown on today's workplaces, which I argue are becoming increasingly transactional and dehumanized. Our 'always on' culture means that stress-related absence is growing and we have normalized overwork. Career burnout is now a recognized phenomenon. Consequently, I make a plea for us to recalibrate our attitudes both towards our work and towards each other. Since working people are likely to spend as much time with their colleagues as they do with family members, it is more important than ever for leaders, line managers and colleagues to understand how to respond to individual suffering and to relate to each other with compassion.

In Chapter 3, I introduce and explain the concepts of self-compassion and compassion for others and also present the business case for compassion. In this chapter, I present the relationship between compassion and business performance and argue that compassion is the hidden heart of strategic advantage.[3] This chapter explains how, in workplaces where compassion is both espoused and embedded, organizations have been found to report superior financial performance, increased innovation, improved collaboration and teamwork, higher levels of customer service and customer advocacy, and increased levels of engagement and retention among staff.

Chapter 4 outlines the deleterious effect on individuals who are going through a difficult life experience when they are not met with compassion from their employer. This chapter contains four real-life short stories of suffering at work, with each one highlighting an area that repeatedly emerges in organizations where compassion is lacking. They are problems with line managers, inflexible HR policies, poor communication from senior management and misguided colleagues.

With the rise in remote working and an increased reliance on technology to communicate, opportunities to physically connect with one another are diminishing. Against this backdrop, many of us possess only a superficial understanding of our colleagues and we often have no idea what challenges people around us may be facing in their lives outside work. Consequently, in Chapter 5, I discuss the importance of human moments. This chapter explores how our relationships at work can be deepened and strengthened when we have the courage to show vulnerability and to talk about our suffering. This chapter also explains the importance of the context in which our disclosures take place and the readiness of our colleagues to hear our struggles, which can make or break human moments at work.

Chapter 6 describes the ways in which individuals report personal growth at work as a result of a difficult life experience. If we are able to create 'safe spaces' in which individuals can talk about their struggles, those conversations can become catalysts for professional development, leading to outcomes such as increased resilience and more compassionate ways of managing others. This chapter suggests that if we give individuals the time and space to self-reflect, with the support of others, the culmination of this is heightened self-awareness, which lies at the heart of effective performance.

Human moments take place spontaneously every day in organizations when someone feels moved to support a colleague in distress. However, for compassion to become consistent and embedded, it needs to be part of an organization's DNA. Consequently, Chapter 7 suggests that there are four pillars of organizational compassion: organizational culture, leadership, social networks, and systems and practices. These pillars are discussed and brought alive using examples from well-known companies such as Cisco, Innocent Drinks, Philips and Nandos.

Chapter 8 presents three case studies of consciously compassionate companies whose representatives were specifically interviewed for this book. Each company is embedding compassion into its culture, leadership, social networks, and systems and practices. From Yodel, a UK-based parcel delivery business with a workforce of 10,000; to Outpost VFX, a visual effects company with around 150 employees; to The Interior Design Partnership, a micro-business with only ten staff, each of these organizations has a different story to tell. By featuring companies of different sizes, ownership structures and industry sectors, this chapter aims to help leaders from a variety of organization types who are looking to transform their own businesses to become consciously compassionate.

The concluding chapter presents eight practical lessons to help line managers, HR professionals and colleagues to better support suffering at work. These lessons include the importance of leaders in setting the tone and context for compassion, which may mean leaders being willing to show their own vulnerability by talking openly about their struggles. This chapter also explains the importance of line managers in making or breaking compassion at work, as well as highlighting the importance of treating people as individuals and flexing around their needs and desires, the role of work in the coping process, and the importance of investing in training and development when it comes to fostering compassion at work.

2

**WHERE DID IT
ALL GO WRONG?**

A few months ago, I boarded a busy commuter train to travel home at the end of a workday. People were crammed into the carriages, occupying all seats and floor space, so, when the conductor spoke over the tannoy system to apologize for the overcrowding, his words were met with rolling eyes and looks of indignation – reactions we have come to expect, perhaps, from long-suffering commuters who regularly face the fallout of an ageing British rail infrastructure.

As a not-so-regular commuter, however, it was the reactions of my fellow travellers towards another human being that shocked and depressed me that evening. A passenger, along with her baby and two young children, got on the train just before departure and was confined to standing in a small space by the train doors. Her children were fractious and she appeared exhausted. No one acknowledged this woman's suffering. People simply looked away or avoided eye contact. I offered for her children to take my seat, which she accepted thankfully; however, my offer was met with tuts and sighs and when the children sat down, they received looks of disdain. Their energy and chatter appeared to be an inconvenience.

I was so upset by these reactions that I found myself announcing my shock at the lack of humanity to everyone in the carriage. Many of these passengers must too have been fathers, mothers or grandparents and have experienced the stress of travelling with young children. We are all cut from the same cloth. As human beings, we all suffer, fail or feel inadequate at times. And yet, so often we forget this and find ourselves ignoring the suffering or distress of others. What has gone wrong in our society to mean that we are unable, or unwilling, to recognize the needs of others? Organizations desensitize people in such a way that by the time they board a train to travel home at the end of the workday, they are incapable of showing kindness to other human beings. So many of us have turned our emotional thermometers down in order to cope with the brutality of work life that we have forgotten *how* to feel. As one HR director said to me, "If my team know I'm having a bad day then I've failed."

Our workplaces are becoming increasingly dehumanized. In part, this may be down to a deeply ingrained belief that work pressure ignites our performance. Our preoccupation with success reduces our capacity to notice and care for others. Organizations are so focused on rewarding productivity and output that many have become obsessed with profit over people. We are so busy 'doing' that many of us have no time to care for ourselves, let alone our colleague down the corridor. We have normalized overwork. Being first in and last out of the office continues to carry a badge of honour in certain industries, with some firms boasting the provision of onsite dentists, physiotherapists, laundry services, late-night food deliveries and 'sleeping pods', so that employees need not go home. Ironically, a recent review promotes these 'perks' as helping to "keep trainees in tip top shape".[4]

The death in 2013 of a young City of London intern who, according to one media report, "worked day and night in the weeks before his death"[5] sparked an overhaul of working practices in some City firms. In Japan, a 24-year-old advertising agency employee committed suicide after clocking up over 100 hours of overtime in the month that preceded her death. Burning the midnight oil is so common in Japan that the Japanese have created a word to describe death by overwork – *karōshi*.[6] And Americans are even worse: US workers have been found to suffer more stress-related illnesses as a result of their long-hours culture than their British or Japanese counterparts.[7]

No wonder global employee engagement levels are so low. Depressingly, only one in seven of us gets up in the morning and looks forward to going to work. In Gallup's 2017 *State of the Global Workplace* report, only 15% of people across 155 countries were found to be engaged, with the lowest levels of engagement reported in China, Japan, South Korea and Taiwan.[8] This is partially due to the traditions of hierarchy in East Asia, where command-and-control approaches to leadership continue to dominate. Employees in this region may also feel they have a poor work-life balance and that there is not enough time to spend with their families given the region's minimal statutory leave provision. In China, employees are entitled to a paltry five days of annual leave, but only after a year of continuous service with their employer.[9]

However, despite having less hierarchy, a focus on work-life balance and more collaborative management practices, Western Europe falls immediately behind East Asia at the bottom of global rankings of employee engagement. In Italy and France, only 5% to 6% of workers describe themselves as engaged. Among the 18 European countries surveyed, the UK ranks in the bottom quartile, reporting some of the highest levels of active disengagement in Europe.[10] Actively disengaged employees are damaging to organizations as they tend to be very vocal about their unhappiness, they monopolize managers' time and they experience the highest rates of absenteeism. Globally, employees are most highly engaged in North America and Latin America; however, with engagement levels of 31% and 27% respectively,[11] there is still much room for improvement.

If we are able to understand why global employee engagement levels are so low and figure out what we can do to improve them, we can potentially transform the world of work. If we feel cared for and valued at work, and if we have strong relationships with our colleagues, we are more likely to be engaged. Developing and fostering compassion could be the key to reviving a disenchanted workforce. Even more striking is that when employees feel engaged in their work, they are more than three times as likely to be thriving in their lives overall than those who are actively disengaged.[12] Despite a widespread recognition by employers of poor engagement among their staff, many companies continue to reward long-hours cultures and promote competition between individuals to get ahead.

For many, this drives workplace behaviours where the showing and sharing of emotions are perceived to be inappropriate. The importance of relating with kindness to our overall sense of wellbeing, both in our personal lives and in our work, cannot be underestimated; however, compassion is often seen as out of bounds within a professional context. Organizations are emotional arenas, yet we display little emotion at work. As a recent discussion paper explains:

> Talking about kindness in a professional context does not sit comfortably with many of us. On a personal level, we fear getting involved in difficult situations, of being asked to give too much, or of being seen as needy.[13]

To survive in our professional contexts, we find ways of coping, one being self-anaesthesia. To be 'professional' is to be tight-lipped. As one manager told me, "We have to be professional and put our emotions in a box." Instead of owning up to our struggles, many of us project a facade of positivity, believing this is what our organization wants to see. We all automatically deliver an "I'm fine" response when someone asks how we are. "What else am I going to say?" said the same manager. Despite our best efforts, it is impossible to compartmentalize our suffering. We may mask our struggles for a while, but they inevitably spill over, affecting our energy, concentration, relationships and morale at work. With more people now living alone and relatives being geographically dispersed, loneliness is becoming one of the most pressing social issues of our generation. It has been found that 22% of Americans and 23% of British people describe themselves as feeling lonely, with campaigns to tackle loneliness being launched in Australia, Denmark and the UK.[14] In an attempt to seek out human connections, people are spending more time at work than they do at home. Never have we needed our colleagues so much, yet never have we felt so isolated, with one in six of us feeling we have no one to talk to at work about the things that worry us.[15] With a rise in remote working and virtual teamwork, our reliance on technology as a means of communication means that human moments at work are becoming lost. Opportunities to physically connect with our colleagues are diminishing and the quality of our networks is being weakened. Workplace loneliness has a destructive effect on both our wellbeing and our job performance.[16] It is line managers who can play the most important role in supporting employees in this regard, but they need to feel they have the capabilities and skills to do so. In a recent study, only 24% of managers had received any mental health training in the past year.[17] As the aforementioned discussion paper puts it:

> There is a growing body of evidence that consistently shows that positive relationships and kindness are at the very heart of our wellbeing. This rings true in our own lives; it is so often our families and friends that bring us warmth and support, who are there in times of need. The absence of these relationships in our own lives, and the lives of others, leads to isolation and loneliness. We are not alone in commenting on loneliness as one of the great 'social evils' of our times.[18]

Faced with increasing volumes of work and the expectations that come with instant communication, many of us carry high levels of cortisol in our bodies just to keep going. Cortisol is often termed the 'stress hormone' because it is released into the body to give us a quick burst of energy in response to stress. Cortisol plays an important physiological role in regulating blood pressure and helping insulin release for example; however, too much cortisol, such as following a period of chronic stress, can be bad for our health. Our 'always on' work culture means that we may be exposing ourselves to damaging levels of cortisol. Not only that, exhaustion has become the new normal and stress-related absence and career burnout are now recognized phenomena. Take the high-profile case of António Horta-Osório, CEO of Lloyds Banking Group, who was signed off with exhaustion only weeks after taking up his position.[19] At the time, both he and the bank refused to say that his absence was stress related, but since then, Horta-Osório has spoken openly about his struggles[20] and has become a high-profile advocate of ending the taboo around mental health at work.[21] Despite some progress being made to destigmatize mental health at work, such as the Time to Change campaign,[22] 12 million adults in the UK seek support from their doctor for mental health issues each year[23] and the World Health Organization estimates that depression affects over 300 million people worldwide.[24] Workplace absence will cost the UK economy £26 billion each year by 2030, with a major contributor being a rise in mental health issues associated with work and family pressures.[25]

So, how can we change this sad reality? By making time for a human moment. A human moment is simply making the time each day to connect with someone at a basic human level and asking them how they are, not because we are being polite or because we are on autopilot. Connecting with someone at a basic human level means being genuinely interested in their response, listening without judgment, and being open and attentive to whatever experiences they may share.

Let me illustrate this with an example. The Parkrun movement is a series of free five-kilometre run events that take place every Saturday morning at 1,400 locations in 23 countries across five continents. Parkruns are free to enter and open to all. Each week, people run, jog or walk five kilometres, with wheelchair users, pensioners, parents and children all taking part side by side. It was at one of these events that I experienced my most recent human moment. I was walking our dog around the course while my daughter and husband ran. During my walk, I came across an elderly man who was dressed as a runner but who was struggling to walk. I quickly caught up with him and we walked together for a while. The man told me about his passion for marathon running. He had run over a hundred marathons in his life, but now he was finding it difficult just to put one foot in front of the other. He talked about how hard it was to walk these days, how he struggles with ageing and how bereft he feels now running is no longer part of his life. To make himself feel better, he gets up every Saturday morning and dresses to run, just so he can feel like a marathon runner once again and be alongside runners as they all come past. I was incredibly moved by his story and felt a deep sense of appreciation for his disclosure. This was a human moment.

Human moments can happen anywhere, at any time, we just need to be open to them. They are now a workplace imperative, in order to prevent organizations from becoming so pressured and so brutal that by the time people board a train to travel home at the end of their workday, they are incapable of showing kindness to another human being. The next time you ask someone at the photocopier how they're doing, if you ask with compassion and without judgment, you just might open up a space for something other than an "I'm fine" response. Chapters 3 onwards explain the generative nature of spontaneous human moments like these and the deleterious effect on individuals when compassion is lacking. First, however, we must come to understand what compassion is and why there is a strong business case for compassion at work. And as the following quote warns, it is needed now more than ever:

> Human beings have come to a point where they no longer know why they exist. They don't use their brains and they have forgotten the secret knowledge of their bodies, their senses, or their dreams. They don't use the knowledge the spirit has put into every one of them ... so they stumble along blindly on the road to nowhere – a paved highway which they themselves can bulldoze and make smooth so they can get faster to the big empty hole which they'll find at the end, waiting to swallow them up.[26]

**COMPASSION
EXPLAINED**

Perhaps so many of us have become caught up in the pursuit of material benefits and financial rewards brought about by career success that we have allowed our capacity to show love, kindness and generosity both to ourselves and others to become lost or forgotten. In a task-focused, performance-driven world of work, it is perhaps laughable to suggest that we add to our to-do list to make time each day to connect with our colleagues. However, when we are on our death beds, not many of us will wish that we had worked more. More often than not, our dying regret will be to have lived a life that was truer to ourselves, rather than having lived a life that others expected of us; to have maintained the friendships that nurture and sustain us; to have given ourselves permission to be happier; or to have had the courage to express our feelings. As one end-of-life patient lamented:

> Why do we depend so much on the material world to validate us? The chase for more, and the need to be recognized through our achievements and belongings, can hinder us from the real things, like time with those we love, time doing things we love ourselves, and balance [in our lives].[27]

If we are able to develop and foster compassion both for ourselves and others, this presents us with a unique opportunity to revive a much-disenchanted workforce. There is growing evidence that self-kindness and positive relationships lie at the heart of our wellbeing, engagement and performance at work.[28] Compassion is fast becoming a business imperative, since it is not money or career success that makes us happy. It is the relationships we have with friends, colleagues and loved ones that are the key to life satisfaction.[29] Close social bonds help us to cope with life's ups and downs; they slow down our mental and physical decline and are better predictors of life expectancy and happiness than class, IQ and genes combined.[30]

That said, self-compassion and compassion for others is often labelled as too 'touchy-feely' and is quickly disregarded in business, with many managers believing that showing too much kindness is weak leadership and instead role-model toughness and strength. When speaking to CEOs, HR directors and managers, they balk at the word 'compassion', describing it as 'cringey', 'soft' or 'overly emotional', and instead prefer more palatable terms such as 'supportive', 'caring' or 'friendly'. But even then, for many, compassion is seen as 'soft and fluffy' and an anathema to the boardroom.

Despite the push-back from some business leaders, compassion is key to preventing stress-related absence and career burnout from becoming the next public health crises. For us to develop genuine compassion towards others, however, we must first develop the capacity to connect with our own feelings and to care for our own welfare. Self-compassion is the first step in work environments that ask a great deal of us, such as the caring professions, otherwise we risk serious damage to our own health and wellbeing.

For instance, a nurse working in a complex care ward recently talked to me about the damaging emotional impact of not being able to attend to her own welfare, because her job demands she make care for others her priority:

> I always put the patient first. I treat my patients as if they are family, because that's how I would want my Mum or Dad to be treated when they are in hospital. I put that image in my mind when I look after them. I treat them like they are my own parents. I give my all to make sure they are comfortable. That's a challenge, though. It's a really big challenge, because we're being stretched and stretched and stretched to the extent where there's a high sickness level, because people are just burning themselves out. People say to me, "How do you do it? How do you manage to smile through it?" and I say, "What can you do?" Because at the end of the day, it's not their fault they're here. But when I go home, I feel really down because I've lost all my energy, all my love and everything and sometimes I can't even smile at my own kids.[31]

Self-compassion is the first step in being able to foster compassion for others. It is the workplace equivalent of being on an aeroplane and being instructed to put on your own oxygen mask before helping others. As a manager, leader or colleague, we are no use to anyone else if we do not first attend to ourselves. First and foremost, self-compassion is about giving ourselves permission to step back and reflect on our own mental, physical and emotional health.

Current work environments are stressful, but we can take steps to develop self-compassion by becoming more aware of how things are for us. Rather than suppressing our pain or beating ourselves up with self-criticism when we fail, fall short or feel inadequate, self-compassion is about developing kindness towards ourselves in these moments. It is not about judging our mental, physical or emotional health, but instead about building a capacity to notice our thoughts and feelings.[32] When we are facing difficulties, we can feel an irrational sense of isolation, as if we are the only person in the world who is struggling. However, self-compassion is also about recognizing that suffering is an inevitable part of the human condition and something that we will all face at times in our lives.[33] The practice of self-compassion has been shown to increase our wellbeing and self-acceptance, as well as to reduce levels of self-criticism.[34] Research also suggests that compassion is the basis of positive influencing skills at work. Bringing warmth to our interactions with others helps us to connect with those around us, demonstrating that we care, we understand and we can be trusted.[35] However, compassion towards others is about more than just an understanding and caring workplace. It is about awakening the emotions within us, so that when we notice that someone is struggling, we try to do something to help.[36] It involves sensing what might be causing someone distress and deciding what might be helpful for them in that moment. Compassion is about taking thoughtful action.[37] It is more than sympathy or empathy. Empathy is when we try to put ourselves in someone else's shoes in order to understand their struggles, or when we feel concern for a colleague who is going through a difficult time.[38] Compassion goes one step further than empathy and is about taking action. We show compassion when we feel compelled to do something to try and alleviate distress. In short, compassion is humanity at work.[39]

Acts of compassion can be small, spontaneous gestures of kindness or company-wide co-ordinated responses to suffering. Take the example of someone in your team whom you have noticed has been working late on a project for several nights in a row. A spontaneous act of compassion might be to tell them to go home early and for you to agree to pick up the strain in order to get the project over the finish line. Company-wide acts of compassion emerge when employees collectively experience trauma, such as the death of a colleague, and there is a culture that enables compassion to flourish. For example, I was confidentially told by the representative of a UK-based energy supplier that when an engineer was killed in service, his colleagues pulled together and helped each other to complete their workloads so that the whole of his workplace could attend his funeral.

When compassion is company-wide, there are systems and practices in place to ensure it is rooted within the organizational culture, so that approaches to recruitment, development and reward reflect genuine care for people. Compassion requires leaders to role-model kindness in their behaviours and for the connections between people to be strong, so that networks can be mobilized to provide support. (The building blocks of corporate compassion are discussed in more detail in Chapter 7.) Compassion is not just about feeling good by doing good.

It also builds the bottom line,[40] having a profound effect on business performance, and is in many ways the hidden heart of strategic advantage.[41] Organizations that are built around the value of compassion have been found to generate better financial performance and experience high levels of employee and customer retention,[42] and this is due to the fact that employees give more because they feel cared for.

It could be argued that nowhere is the business case for compassion more important than in healthcare, where the attitudes of employees can directly affect the quality of the patient experience. Research in the health sector in the UK has connected compassion to a variety of individual and organizational performance outcomes. For example, in NHS trusts with consciously compassionate work cultures, employees are more likely to feel they can speak up to report errors or problems, and collaboration and innovation improve, as does the overall quality of patient care.[43] Furthermore, in NHS trusts that prioritize compassionate leadership, this has been found to improve the health, wellbeing and engagement of all staff. For example, since 2009, the NHS has been running a staff survey whereby all NHS trusts in England are sent a questionnaire that asks employees about their experience at work. Data collected through the NHS Staff Survey has found that when staff do not feel cared for and are disengaged, this has a damaging impact on a range of performance outcomes, such as increased staff absenteeism, higher infection rates in patients and higher rates of patient mortality. Simply put, in these work environments, compassion is a matter of life or death.[44]

It is not only when times are good that compassion is important for business. Research on the handling of dismissals and redundancies shows that if they are done compassionately, through sensitive and careful communication, outplacement support and generous severance packages – this can positively influence an employee's perception of the organization long after they have left.[45] Furthermore, companies that explicitly put their people before profits when times are tough – by resisting layoffs, for example – have been found to perform better in the long term as their employees work harder and are more committed to helping their employer recover from the crisis by repaying the loyalty shown to them during tough times.[46]

Gestures of compassion can also have a great impact on customer advocacy.[47] Research has shown that customer retention and loyalty are not created by price, promotions or loyalty schemes but by the care and emotion shown by the company's employees.[48] People stay loyal to brands or organizations when they capture their trust and deeply felt affection, which is why Gallup, for example, measures loyalty in terms of a customer's 'emotional attachment' to a brand.[49] This can be instilled through gestures of compassion, such as the often-told example of when a business traveller arrived at one of Ritz-Carlton's hotels over seven hours late after a series of delayed flights. She was greeted by an understanding Ritz-Carlton employee who offered to book her into their spa to help her to relax. The customer explained she was too tired to visit the spa, so instead the employee brought her a scented candle to help her relax. The woman was so touched by this gesture that she told the hotel staff on checkout how moved she had been by the act of kindness. This story was shared and celebrated across Ritz-Carlton as well as being logged in the company's customer database, so whenever the customer checks into any of its hotels, she is presented with a scented candle in her room. All Ritz-Carlton employees are trained to notice, care, think and act thoughtfully for its customers; they call this attitude the 'Ritz-Carlton Mystique'.[50]

My husband and I experienced this phenomenon first-hand during our honeymoon to Mauritius when, on a boat trip to a nearby beach, a storm washed away our daysacks containing our clothes, money and mobile phones. Unbeknown to us, the hotel was told about the incident by the boat crew and, when we returned to our room at dusk, feeling bedraggled and tired, the housekeeping staff had run us a foamy bath covered in fresh flowers. We were so touched by their thoughtful act of compassion that we wrote to the hotel manager to express our gratitude. We have since shared this story many times with our friends and work colleagues and plan to return to the same hotel in the future. By transforming problems into opportunities, organizations can delight their customers and drive customer loyalty, as was the case on our honeymoon. In fact, research shows that in many cases, companies that deal with problems quickly and with care tend to engender customer passion and loyalty just as well as those companies whose customers never encountered a problem in the first place.[51]

It takes a focus by the organization on the development of its people to become skilled at noticing, thinking and acting thoughtfully for its customers and, in turn, employees need to see the same treatment towards themselves. Unsurprisingly, then, caring managers and caring colleagues have been found to be two of the most important predictors of employee performance.[52] To the cynical among us, compassion may simply be seen as a subverted way of getting more from employees; however, the leaders and managers who fail to display genuine care are easily spotted and people ultimately speak with their feet. As the old adage goes, people leave managers, not jobs. Notwithstanding this cynicism, if we care about each other as human beings, compassion at work is a basic requirement and the ability to exercise 'competent compassion' a key professional skill.[53]

Acting with compassion is not easy, however. It requires courage and sometimes it can mean challenging industry norms or the unquestioned assumptions within our workplaces about what it is acceptable to show or share when it comes to our feelings. Organizations are emotional arenas and all of our interactions at work generate emotional responses in us. Most organizations, however, possess 'feeling rules' in which people are expected to put on a mask or a brave face at work and say they are 'fine' no matter how they are feeling. A recent example of this came up in a conversation with a manager who told me that he believed it was his job to display strength to his direct reports at all times. When he is going through a difficult time at work, he feels it is his responsibility to "grin through the pain" if that is what is required, so that he can pretend to be upbeat to try and keep everybody else happy. Organizations that promote open and honest emotional exchanges build connections and understanding between people and ultimately help employees to act with compassion towards one another as well as towards their customers or clients. However, as the stories in the next chapter show, sadly, these kinds of organization are few and far between. It is difficult to find examples of consciously compassionate companies, as the norm is a focus on productivity and output, or profit over people, which means in many organizations compassion has no place at work.

4

WHEN
COMPASSION
IS LACKING

At some point in our lives, it is inevitable that we will face a difficult life experience, be it separation or divorce, family breakdown or the death of a loved one. For example, take the onset of a critical illness. According to Cancer Research UK, 50% of the population will be diagnosed with cancer during their lifetime.[54] As people work longer and retire later, the number of people affected by illness and bereavement is set to rise exponentially within the next few decades. Despite our best efforts, it is impossible to keep the pain and angst brought about by these experiences separate from our professional lives. The 'suffering overspill' caused by the difficulties we face in our home life inevitably affects our motivation, performance and relationships at work, yet employers know little about how to respond.[55] Working people spend as much time with their colleagues as they do with family members; therefore, the way in which we support individuals both formally (through company policies and procedures) and informally (as colleagues and friends) is a critical business issue. Unfortunately, examples of consciously compassionate companies are few and far between. For compassion to be 'organized',[56] it requires a company culture that is conducive for it to flourish and the systems in place to embed culture within its practices. In consciously compassionate cultures, leaders role-model kindness, and the connections between employees across the organization are strong. Sadly, these kinds of organization are the exception rather than the rule. Each of the stories that follow sheds a light on the areas that repeatedly emerge in organizations where compassion is lacking, including line management, HR, senior leadership and colleagues.

THE UNSYMPATHETIC BOSS

Diane[57] is in her 50s. She works as a senior manager in a not-for-profit organization in the southeast of England. Diane requested that information about the nature of her role and organization remain confidential, so that neither she nor her employer could be identified. Diane suffered a double bereavement, losing both her sister and her father to cancer in the same week. In an initial conversation with her boss, when she relayed the news of her sister's death following the death of her father, instead of receiving genuine empathy and care, Diane felt an underlying pressure to return to work as soon as possible:

> [My boss said], "Oh well, you're not coming back on Monday then?" and it was like, "No! Hello?! My sister has just died now as well as my father and it's going to be another week before we can organize a funeral." I remember feeling annoyed. I wasn't annoyed at the fact that he was making the right noises – he was making all the right noises, [saying things like] "it's very sad" and everything – but I got this underlying sense of pressure and I thought it was really inappropriate. I was so annoyed. If he had pushed it in any way at all I'd have probably just said I'm not coming back – I'm handing in my notice right now.

Diane felt that a prolonged absence from work would be viewed negatively. She said:

I was worried for my job because lots of people were being made redundant. There was a lot of change going on, and I didn't want to give people any excuse.

Diane suffered in silence and did not talk about her anxieties. She worked in an environment where she did not feel it was safe to share her feelings, which is common in her experience. She explained:

There are few organizations where you can talk in a safe way without being seen as difficult. In the workplace, you have to choose your words very carefully.

On her return to work, despite being under huge psychological strain, she felt a pressure to maintain her professionalism and to keep up the appearance of a high-performing senior manager:

When people asked me how I was, maybe some of them did have genuine care, but I said, "I'm fine" because what else was I going to say? Actually, "No, I think I'm going mad?!"

Without being able to openly express her emotions at work, her grief became "stifled"[58] and her emotion surfaced inappropriately. Through her attempt to try to suppress her grief at work, the grief became displaced anger. With no outlet for her grief, Diane's anger started to show up in meetings and in her exchanges with her boss and colleagues:

Everyone around me was collapsing. At home my mum was in a terrible state. She was not coping. My brother was having a nervous breakdown, and my husband was almost on the verge of one, and I had to go in and do my job. What would happen if I fell apart? I couldn't do that, and luckily, it's not in me to completely fall apart. In many ways, it was better for me to be at work rather than thinking about it. It was when I had moments to myself that I got very upset. I remember being very angry all of the time and sometimes not being able to hide it very well. It would pop up every now and again. I remember being very irritated with people and being on quite a short fuse. Basically, I was really pissed off about everything and everyone.

Diane's boss noticed her angry outbursts but, instead of seeking to understand the grieving process, he labelled her behaviour as "turbulent". If he had truly understood Diane and the strain she was under, he might have thought to offer her an opportunity to talk in confidence about her concerns or suggest that she seek external professional support. Instead, Diane's struggles were picked up months later by her GP, as at work any grief talk was off limits between Diane and her line manager. She said:

I think that [my manager] found it embarrassing, and I honestly don't think he knew how to deal with it at all. If I wanted to talk in any depth it was really just about getting the job done.

When I asked him about his recollections of these events, Diane's boss related that he had experienced the sudden loss of a parent himself, but he described himself as "hardened" rather than more empathetic as a result of his own experience. He remembered that he did not respond to Diane with compassion because he felt he had "a level of indignation about it", having not received care and support following the death of his mother. He also reflected that he was "driven and demanding" at the time despite Diane's emotional fragility at work. There were limits to the support he offered Diane, because in his mind "there was a job to be done".

Recent research has found that, like Diane's boss, two thirds of line managers put the interests of the organization before their own staff wellbeing, with 12% of them doing so every day.[59] This may be because individuals or their line managers view grief as off limits and not the organization's business. In the UK, the 'stiff upper lip' culture still prevails in many workplaces, where people are expected to hide their personal issues. This means, as in Diane's case, suffering frequently remains hidden. Line managers often do not know their team members well enough to be able to pick up on the underlying signs of grief, such as a loss of confidence, decreased motivation or increased irritability – nor do they have the contextual knowledge of their direct reports' home lives needed to understand their triggers. This makes it a minefield for managers who lack the adequate training or support to know how to raise the subject of suffering among their staff, or to address suffering once it has surfaced.

THE POLICY POLICE

A few years ago, at the age of 33, Bill was diagnosed with leukaemia. At the time, he was employed by a large healthcare company based in the UK. He worked in learning and development and his role involved the line management of seven people. Bill's diagnosis meant that he spent over six months undergoing chemotherapy, which involved a series of one- to two-month stays in hospital during that period. Most of Bill's illness was spent within the confines of hospital without any of the normal social interactions that happen in the outside world. His illness was a frightening and solitary experience. The interactions between Bill and his colleagues at the time, particularly those in his HR department, were poorly handled, which caused him additional stress during this difficult period in his life. Not only was Bill impaired by an initial lack of information from his hospital consultants about his diagnosis but also the initial shock of the diagnosis prevented him from being able to think straight or to communicate effectively with his company's HR department. He recounted:

> I remember thinking, I don't know how to word this, how to put this across, how to manage this conversation.

Bill's exchanges with his HR department provoked fear and uncertainty, and he felt that none of these interactions were conducted with any sensitivity or compassion. He remembered his dealings with HR as 'box-ticking' exercises, such as a visit from a welfare officer who was sent out of the blue by his employer during his illness. He recalled:

> I remember being concerned that he [the welfare officer] was coming to see if I was still ill enough to be off work. Looking back in hindsight that was a ridiculous thought, but I remember thinking he was like the illness police.

This impromptu visit was anxiety provoking on several levels. Firstly, Bill felt he was being assessed in some way, since the HR department had neither consulted him beforehand nor given him any background as to the purpose of the visit. If asked, Bill would have opted for a phone call, rather than an in-person visit, as he found it extremely distressing at the time for people from work to see him while he was undergoing chemotherapy as he did not want them to see him "in that state". However well intentioned, the visit from the welfare officer left Bill feeling suspicious of his organization. He said:

> They're still the employer, and I wondered if in the back of their minds they were thinking, "If this doesn't go the right way, we'll have to terminate for sickness." There's always that edge with your employer, and I think I was always conscious of that.

Secondly, the behaviours exhibited by some staff in the HR department added undue anxiety at a time when Bill was at his most vulnerable. In another incident, in blind pursuit of policy compliance, someone from the HR team telephoned him during his chemotherapy treatment to tell him that they had discovered a two-day gap in his sickness forms. They requested that he complete and return a new form to cover the two missing days. Looking back, this request seems unbelievably insensitive:

> When you're lying in bed and you can't move and you see the consultant twice a week and your brain is completely fuzzy and you're in a complete mess emotionally, even though you probably don't realize it, and you're just trying to sort out what is going on in terms of your treatment, the concept of filling in and signing a form is actually quite difficult.

Bill wanted to "do the right thing" and stay in HR's "good books" as he had been off sick for an extended period and because he felt guilty for being off work, but his organization did not appear to seek to understand or empathize with his situation at the time. No attempt was made by HR to connect with Bill at a basic human level, to find out how he was coping and to see whether there was anything the organization could do to help. His only interactions with the HR team at the time were around sickness policy compliance. Bill had just bought his first home, so when his sick pay came to an end, he had no choice but to return to work as HR announced in a letter to him that he would be dropped to half pay. Bill explained:

I had no savings and no backup. There were a couple of things I was worried about – one was going onto half pay. How am I going to pay the mortgage? The second was that I was really conscious that after having nine months off, if somehow I didn't perform at work and they sacked me, I couldn't then get another job because I'd just had nine months off and therefore how would I get an income and how would I pay the mortgage? This really started playing on my mind.

Looking back, Bill's interactions with his employer seem deeply ironic given that he worked for a healthcare organization in a learning and development role. Rumours spread in the organization at the time about the handling of Bill's sick leave, with HR's strict adherence to policy being seen as deeply uncompassionate. One of his colleagues said:

They get you onto half pay if they think it's about time you came back and that encourages you to get back quicker.

People in the organization questioned whether inflexibilities in the sickness-pay policy had forced Bill to return to work prematurely and several people blamed HR for the "distress" Bill suffered. It was suggested that the constant 'red tape' had made the process feel administrative and transactional, which had prevented the organization from being able to provide Bill with tailored and personal support. One colleague lamented:

It was a bad phase in the company and unfortunately this was when Bill was at his most vulnerable.

Questions still remain as to whether the company learned anything from Bill's experience. Neither he nor any of his colleagues that I spoke to remained at the company. All of them subsequently left.

COMMUNICATION BREAKDOWN

Edgar is 41 years old. He works as a sales director for a UK-based, privately owned magazine marketing business. He has been with the company for 15 years. At the time of our conversations, Edgar had just undergone nine months of treatment for kidney cancer, which involved an initial operation to remove a 14-centimetre tumour from his kidney, liver and diaphragm and then subsequent chemotherapy. Edgar and his colleagues viewed their employer's handling of his illness very differently. His colleagues talked of his illness being "mishandled", particularly his transition back to work. They distinguished between spontaneous expressions of love, support and compassion that he received from his colleagues and a lack of formal support offered by the company board. As one colleague said:

> The organization didn't seem to do a lot, but individuals within the company did.

Edgar's recollections partially aligned with those of his colleagues, as he said he had "felt the love" from them, which he believed had helped to give him the strength he needed to fight the cancer. However, in contrast to his colleagues, his view of his company's handling of his illness was entirely positive. He said he had felt in control when it came to communicating with the rest of the organization about his diagnosis, since the members of the board had not only asked his permission to inform staff when he was initially diagnosed but also asked how much detail they should reveal about his illness. Edgar said he appreciated that senior leadership had taken such a close interest in his wellbeing from the outset, and he continuously received reassurances from members of the board during his time off work. He returned to work early while his treatment was ongoing (a decision that he took himself in order to try to regain some normality), and he talked positively about the way his company had managed this transition:

> I truly believe that the company were helping me. They were looking out for me, they cared about me and they were not just fulfilling their obligation as part of an HR policy or [in line with] legislation – and that's what made a difference. It made it genuine.

Unfortunately, Edgar's colleagues did not see the organization's handling of his illness in the same way. His decision to return to work while treatment was ongoing was part of his coping strategy. He believed that if he re-established some work projects, this might bring a sense of normality and routine to a world that was otherwise in disarray. However, without any formal communication about the reasons behind his return, either by Edgar himself or by the board, rumour became established fact. This lack of communication backfired and people presumed the worst: there was a widespread assumption at all levels within the company that he had been forced back to work. Employees began to "bitch" about his perceived poor treatment and their ensuing belief that he had been prematurely forced back. They divided themselves into 'us' (the people who cared) and 'them' (senior leadership who didn't care about Edgar's welfare) and began a metaphorical fight with "those bastards upstairs".

Prior research has shown that if people are treated with compassion, they are more likely to stay in the organization longer and work harder for their employer.[60] This is also true for employees who witness their colleagues being treated with compassion. But the opposite is also true. If we witness a lack of care being shown to our colleagues, we question our own commitment to the organization, despite the fact that it is not us who are at the receiving end.[61] This was the case in Edgar's situation, where a lack of communication at his place of work created a shared belief that compassion was lacking. This led several employees to question their commitment to the organization. They decided that the company's response to his illness was representative of the culture writ large. As one colleague bemoaned:

I think there was a moral issue because there were many of us who were thinking, "I've been here for 18 years. I've given 18 years to this company and if that's how they're going to treat you ..." We don't know for sure, that's how it was, so it's one of those gossiping, bitching situations. A group of people here all thinking, "Those bastards upstairs aren't looking after him."

MISGUIDED COLLEAGUES

Richard is in his mid-50s. He works for a domestic housebuilding and construction company. He has worked as a project manager in this organization for over 25 years and manages a team of five people. Ten years ago, Richard's eldest child, who was a teenager at the time, died in a motorcycle accident. Having worked in the same organization for over 25 years, Richard's sense of identity is bound up in his work. He described himself to me as much more comfortable managing projects and deliverables than dealing with people or emotions. In the immediate aftermath of his son's death, Richard took little time off and literally tried to "work through it". His work became a way of coping, as it brought him much-needed daily structure and routine. Despite his colleagues being aware of his tragedy, Richard did not talk to anyone at work about what he was going through. He was fiercely private and strove to keep his work and home lives separate. He talked to me about work being an important "distraction" at the time. He could go to work to pretend that his life was normal and to temporarily forget. He explained:

It was a relief to have something else to think about rather than the problems at home.

Since Richard did not speak about his bereavement at work, his colleagues could not have known how to support him, yet he remained surprised that no one at work approached him about his loss. Because he stayed silent and did not communicate how he would have liked people to act around him, colleagues were unsure as to whether they should acknowledge his tragedy or not. However, Richard just saw this as "their way of avoiding a difficult situation". His behaviour at work compounded the situation as he said he tried to "put on an act" and was "just going through the motions". Trying to carry on as normal at work was emotionally draining. As he described:

> I was putting on a front, so everything became really laborious and tiring. I was trying to do my normal job but underlying that I was acting all the time and putting on a brave face, so everything became pretty tiring.

Richard admitted to me that in the ten years since his son's death, he has never recovered from some conversations that took place at that time. He remembered a work colleague at a social function soon after his bereavement who joked about hating being a parent to a teenager, because of their mood swings and rudeness. This had been an innocent, throw-away comment, but Richard admitted that he had "never liked the woman since".

Richard experienced the detrimental effects of suppressing his true emotions at work,[62] such as fatigue and insomnia in the short term, and recurring bouts of depression and anxiety over the longer term. However, by not acknowledging the stress he was experiencing, work colleagues remained unaware and therefore unable to provide the support he required:

> People thought I was fine at work. They couldn't see any difference in me, but internally I was feeling the stress and then I would take a nosedive. I would take some time off work, which was normally a couple of weeks. I would go and see the doctor, get on some medication and then I would fade myself back into work because I found it helpful. Within a month I would be back into work full time and would have reset myself.

On the rare occasions when Richard tried to share his personal problems with his colleagues, his disclosures were met with awkwardness because they were seen as out of character. His colleagues were caught off guard and didn't know how to respond. Richard told me about one such interaction:

> When I went into work in that period it was so difficult. I remember seeing one person in the staff coffee area. I was having such a bad day that day, I just blurted out that I was feeling dire and I wasn't coping. I remember her saying dismissively, "Oh well, it can't be as bad as all that," and that was difficult.

Richard failed to connect with this woman because she appeared not to understand his situation or know how to respond. He realized "it wasn't badly intentioned"; however, well-meaning colleagues can be misguided in their attempts to show compassion if there is a superficial understanding of the situation or individual, or there is a lack of knowledge about what to expect from someone who is experiencing grief.[63]

In these instances, misguided acts of compassion can add to a person's distress as opposed to alleviating it. Reactions to disclosures and confessions at work are critical in shaping how someone will deal with their loss.[64] When disclosures are met with judgments or trite statements, they can be detrimental to an individual, especially when, as it was for Richard, work is a way of coping. Without the opportunity to discuss his personal issues, Richard became anxious and depressed. He wanted his colleagues to acknowledge his trauma but, since this was not a need that he expressed, most of his colleagues did not attempt to talk to him about it.

In such instances, grief training can be extremely helpful so that colleagues, line managers and HR professionals can learn how to respond appropriately. Colleagues working alongside individuals who, like Richard, are facing complicated grief or sudden loss should gently acknowledge their trauma and be available should they wish to talk. Being accessible and willing to listen without judgment can often be a simple yet powerful role for colleagues to play. Getting individuals off-site and out of the office can also help, since individuals are much more likely to talk about their struggles outside the work environment, where they will feel less 'on show'.

KEY CONSIDERATIONS

By sharing examples of when things go wrong and compassion is lacking, each of these stories serves to demonstrate some of the key considerations for line managers, leaders, colleagues and HR professionals when dealing with individual suffering at work. The first story illustrates the importance of supportive line managers who understand the grief process when facilitating an individual's transition back to work, and it also demonstrates the need for 'safe spaces' for those people who wish to talk at work about their ongoing struggles. Line managers should be present for the individual, by acknowledging their suffering but without making unrealistic demands on them; be patient with the person concerned, particularly around their performance in the early stages of their return to work; and be open to discussing mortality or mental health as a universal human experience. When line managers are open, it makes it much easier for others to mention these experiences when they happen.[65] The second story illustrates the negative image of HR when there is seen to be a sweeping application of policy without flexibility or consideration of an individual's circumstances or needs. The second story also shows that without clear communication and reassurances, the purpose of home visits from the employer can be misconstrued, particularly when individuals are at their most vulnerable. When it comes to senior leaders, it is important they understand that their words and actions are under the spotlight, with their treatment of those who are going through a difficult life experience being seen as representative of the organization's culture writ large. If someone is perceived to have been unfairly treated by the leaders of an organization, other employees will question their own commitment to the organization as a result. Finally, the importance of training across the organization cannot be underestimated, since gestures of compassion can be misguided if there is a lack of knowledge or understanding of the individual concerned.

5

HUMAN
MOMENTS

One thing that connects us all as human beings is that we allsuffer. Prompted by my own experience, I began to research trauma and compassion at work.[66] Over the past ten years, I have worked with many individuals in organizations to help them think about how their personal life journeys have shaped who they are and how they might have the courage to share their stories with others. By finding the courage to make a personal disclosure about our daily or life struggles, we can create a human moment. Each time I work with people on this topic, I am reminded that human moments can only happen if we have the courage to share. Personal disclosures then open up a space for someone else to disclose their own. As one manager recently said to me:

> You discover how many other people have suffered, but people don't talk about it until they know that you've suffered too.

Our suffering, be it daily struggles or significant life events, provide a platform and legitimacy for people to express their "real feelings" at work.[67] A female professional whom I recently spoke with told me that she had just returned from a period of stress-related absence brought about by an abusive marriage. She had decided to pluck up the courage to tell some of her close colleagues the reasons behind her absence and, after she had done so, her work relationships were transformed. She said:

> They now see me in a completely different way. They see me as the person rather than the professional.

The same person told me she felt overwhelmed by "the amount of love" she got back from her colleagues following her disclosure. One of her colleagues said:

> People find it quite difficult to talk about their struggles as it tends to be a taboo subject at work. Her honesty was refreshing. It is far better than pretending everything is okay.

Acts of disclosure, such as this one, can profoundly strengthen our relationships at work. That said, disclosures of this kind are much more likely to take place outside the work environment, where people feel safe to speak openly. Furthermore, when disclosures are met with an open mind and a readiness to listen, a compassionate connection is made.

CONTEXT IS KEY

Peter is 48 years old. He lives in the Midlands, England, with his wife, son and twin children. He works in IT for a large American engineering company. He has been in the organization for over ten years and manages a team of four people. In 2009, Peter's second child was born critically ill with severe brain damage and cerebral palsy and died six weeks after birth. He found the courage to talk about his situation in settings outside work, where he was more relaxed and out of work mode:

I remember being away on a business trip with the general manager. He had a reputation for being unemotional and a hard businessman, but on the flight home we ended up talking about it, and he ended up relating a similar personal story. This was a bloke who I had a working relationship with, but didn't know him personally, and [he] was prepared to share his own story with me about the death of his sister. I found that really helpful.

Talking about the difficult time he was going through opened a space for Peter's colleague to share his own story, which helped them both to realize they were not alone in their suffering. For Peter, these unplanned and in-the-moment conversations outside work were extremely helpful. A year later, when Peter's wife was once again pregnant, this time with twins, he experienced a similar moment of unexpected human connection when out with a client. He said:

I went out for a meal with a client and for some reason we ended up talking about the twins. I must have said something like, "We're a little bit nervous because of what happened a year ago," and I remember telling the client about it. He was great. He was really sympathetic and when the twins were born, he sent a card and some Babygros for them as a gift. This was a client that I hardly knew. It was a fleeting working relationship over six or nine months, and he was probably more supportive than the people I'd worked with for a decade.

Peter was able to talk about his suffering outside the professional environment, with someone he would only be working with temporarily. He found safety within the anonymity of this relationship. This shows that human moments can happen anywhere and at any time. We just need to be open to them.

COMPASSION TAKES READINESS

Our willingness to show vulnerability and tell our stories not only depends on people being available to listen, whether within or outside work; it also takes a readiness on the part of the listener to be able to hear our pain. Nigel, one of Peter's colleagues, became unwittingly involved in his situation because of a 'sliding doors' moment. After a chance encounter between Peter and Nigel on the doorstep of Peter's home soon after the birth of his critically ill second child, they became deeply connected. Nigel told me:

> It just so happened that I went to Peter's house to congratulate [him and his wife] on the birth of his baby. I wouldn't normally have gone round, but because we lived in the same village, I decided to stop by. I knocked on the door expecting to see the proud father all cheerful and smiles and to go in to congratulate everybody and I never made it past the porch. He said, "I've got all the family in there and we're all a bit distraught. I can't really invite you in." I said, "Why's that?" and then he started to explain everything that had happened. I ended up with

a grown man in tears in my arms on the doorstep, because at that point it was at the height of his shock and trauma. It's quite an experience, because you go from being colleagues to suddenly becoming part of his traumatic experience.

Peter remembered Nigel as a "great support". For him, the doorstep conversation was a human moment. Nigel, however, felt very differently. He believed that because he had unwittingly walked in on Peter's situation and had been unprepared for what he was about to hear, he had been thrust involuntarily into the midst of Peter's trauma. This interaction fundamentally changed the connection between them, with Nigel going from being a colleague to unintendedly becoming a part of Peter's family's trauma. At that point, he knew more than anyone else in the organization about what was going on, but Nigel just wanted to be like everyone else in the office, where a professional distance was maintained. He felt burdened with compassionate responsibility, which was not something he felt ready or equipped for:

Things could have been so different. If I hadn't gone round that night to congratulate them, and I'd found out like everybody else in the office, maybe this would never have happened, and I wouldn't have had that effect on him each time we met, and we could've carried on as normal. But it did happen and that effect does occur, and it's gone on for a very long time. That's the thing that struck me most of all. Just how many years later, and I still have that effect on him.

Nigel began to avoid Peter as he didn't want to trigger his suffering at work. His displays of emotion made Nigel feel uncomfortable, and he felt they should not happen in a professional context. He never talked to Peter about how he felt. He has since moved away, and they are now based in different parts of the UK, no longer working together on a regular basis. It was only by having conversations with both of them that I came to understand how two people can view the same human moment so differently, simply because one person did not feel equipped or ready to offer their support.

Human moments can happen when you least expect them, therefore we need to "ready"[68] ourselves for compassion, which is about developing a capacity to take another person's perspective, which might be very different from our own, and then discern what might be helpful for them in the moment.[69] Getting ourselves "ready" for compassion is also about opening ourselves up for an encounter to unfold. If and when it does, we listen with empathy and without judgment, we acknowledge the other person's experience even if we cannot change it, and we accept that we may need to intuitively feel our way in these interactions without having *the* answer about what is helpful or the right thing to do for that person at that time.

All of the interactions reported in this chapter happened spontaneously, when individuals found themselves in situations in which they felt able to talk. We continue to have a problem in organizations, however, as many people remain reticent about showing their vulnerability and talking about their struggles at work. It takes a first-class "noticer"[70] to pick up on the hidden signs of distress, such as increased tiredness or irritability in a colleague, a direct report who appears withdrawn and less engaged, or an out-of-character emotional outburst in a manager. A certain level of intimacy is required to pick up on the signals of someone behaving differently. Unfortunately, many of us do not know our colleagues very deeply and we generally have a superficial understanding of their lives at home. Through gentle inquiry and by asking questions, rather than making assumptions, we can start to create a safe space for people to talk. But in many workplaces, the social norms are such that the showing and sharing of feelings continue to be seen as out of bounds.

6

LEARNING
THE HARD WAY

They say a problem shared is a problem halved, but human moments are more than opportunities to bring to the surface our struggles in conversation with others. Difficult life events can be key moments of learning and instrumental to our personal growth. It is when our backs are against the wall and we are at the lowest points in our lives that we learn the most about ourselves. With adequate time and support, more often than not, people will derive something positive from their experience. By giving individuals the space to reflect, my research has found that people see themselves as having grown professionally as a result of their experiences and are rated by their colleagues as more effective at work as a result.[71] This is post-traumatic growth, which is a concept that has emerged in recent years from the field of positive psychology. It is the idea that alongside acute distress, many individuals report positive psychological changes following difficult life experiences.[72] Some people talk of increased personal strength – that is to say, a recognition of newfound emotional and psychological skills that help them to deal with adversity. Others talk about discovering a new life path or a new philosophy on life that was not present before. Some people describe changes in their relationships as a result of a traumatic life experience, such as a greater emotional connection with those around them, increased self-disclosure and a recognition that since their experience, some of their social networks have become more meaningful while others have been weakened or have ended. Other people talk about how their life priorities having changed. They no longer sweat the small stuff and have a greater appreciation of the simple things in life, such as taking a walk in nature or witnessing a beautiful sunset. Others talk of increased spirituality or finding faith as a result of going through a difficult life event.

Before my study,[73] all of the research in this field was focused on people working in settings where exposure to trauma is commonplace, such as the emergency services, disaster recovery work or the military. My study was the first of its kind to look at post-traumatic growth among people working in everyday workplaces, that is to say, professionals working in financial services, pharmaceuticals, education, logistics, charities, healthcare or retail, to name a few. Notwithstanding their ongoing pain following a difficult period in their lives, unprompted, these individuals described something positive having come out of their experience. In relation to their attitude towards work specifically, my research uncovered four types of personal growth: appreciation of life, new possibilities, personal strength and managerial growth.

APPRECIATION OF LIFE

In all of the research I have done with individuals following personal trauma, appreciation of life is most often reported. Driven, successful professionals talk about how work was once everything to them, with success being defined in relation to their salary or seniority, but that in the light of what they have been through, and often faced with their own mortality, they gain a new perspective on the relative importance of work.

Following his struggle with cancer, for example, one manager described how it gave him an opportunity to step back and reflect on his work-life balance and to change his priorities when it came to his work. He told me:

> I've probably missed an awful lot of my kids' childhood not being there having dinner with them every night as most other families probably do. I realized I needed to do something about it. Had I not had this opportunity to stop and step back and think about it, it would've been too late.

Peter, whose story was told in the previous chapter, talked to me unprompted about his experience of child bereavement having "put things into perspective". Previously, he had viewed his personal and professional lives as two completely separate things and had endeavoured to keep a divide between them. He would try to leave his personal life at the door when he came to work, believing that he should never discuss his private affairs in public. Then, after his trauma, he realized that "they are really one and the same" and that it is fruitless to attempt to keep one's home and work lives separate since the whole person goes to work.

Whatever is going on for us in our personal lives inevitably affects our motivation, performance and interactions at work. We can only keep a lid on our personal struggles for so long, before they spill over. People I have worked with have often said that a difficult life event gave them permission or legitimacy to become more open about their emotions and experiences; they stopped trying to maintain a personal–professional divide and became more honest about their mental, physical and emotional health at work.

NEW POSSIBILITIES

Following a personal trauma, some people decide that they need a complete career change, and this decision is often connected to the way in which they have been treated by their employer during their difficult life experience. In this situation, people often talk about becoming disillusioned with their place of work, having been treated badly by their employer. This happened to Bill (described in Chapter 4), who chose redundancy and decided to have a complete break from corporate life following his battle with leukaemia. He told me:

> I'm pretty convinced that it all goes back to my situation. I was quite risk averse before. I would have worked to keep the corporate job, whereas I got the opportunity and thought, you know what, I'm going to take that opportunity and just have a break.

Interestingly, when colleagues see someone else being treated badly by their employer when that person is going through a difficult time, these people question their own commitment to the organization as a result.[74] In short, if a lack of care is witnessed by others, this can lead them to reassess their own view of their employer. So, compassion is not only important for the individual themselves but also important for everyone around them. In some instances, when individuals witness the suffering of others, vicarious growth occurs, as they decide life is too short and choose to pursue a new life path for themselves. For example, I once spoke with a woman who worked alongside a colleague who had been diagnosed with stage three breast cancer and who decided to resign from her career in financial services and retrain as a paramedic. In conversation, she told me that her decision had been made as a direct result of witnessing her colleague's battle with cancer. She realized there was no time like the present and decided to leave her current job, go back to university and follow her dream.

PERSONAL STRENGTH

Suffering can also lead to greater self-insight. It is during life's deepest lows that our coping mechanisms and behaviours under pressure are brought into sharp relief. After having lived through something difficult, many people talk about being more in tune with themselves as a result. In these instances, people talk about not realizing how mentally strong they could be until their resources of survival were put to the ultimate test. As a consequence, they describe a newfound psychological strength, which becomes a useful benchmark from which to review their ability to cope with pressure at work. Whereas previously these people may have found themselves struggling to deal with organizational politics, an angry client, or mistakes and failures at work, they now know that these stresses and strains pale into insignificance when it comes to what they have managed to live through.

MANAGERIAL GROWTH

In the research I have conducted over the past decade with leaders and managers who have experienced trauma in their personal lives, without exception, all of them talk about managing others differently as a result of their experience, such as leading with a newfound care and compassion towards their colleagues. Others talk about gaining a new perspective on the relative importance of work, such as deciding that life is too short to get involved in office politics. These people may have previously made sure they were highly visible in the organization by volunteering for committees or special projects, or by sitting on the right tables in the staff canteen; but through a difficult life experience, they come to realize the value of meaningful connections at work and thus prioritize interacting with people whom they genuinely respect and value. Other people talk about being more open about their personal lives and disclosing their feelings and ongoing struggles more readily at work. Colleagues around them describe how this newfound openness helps to create a climate of trust, connection and psychological safety at work, which makes it okay for others to share their struggles too. Some managers have embedded these practices in their teams by introducing the idea of personal time, whereby colleagues are able to come and talk to them at any time about anything (work or non-work related). Others have introduced regular check-ins at the start of team meetings, so that teams begin with non-task talk. Here, team members talk about how they are feeling and what is going on for them personally in that particular week.

Following a personal trauma, some managers talk about adopting a coaching approach to management following their difficult life experience. For them, it becomes less about forging their own career success and more about creating a space for others to grow, by giving them more autonomy, flexibility and stretching opportunities at work. Others talk about having had to learn to 'let go' since they were physically absent from work for an extended period. This situation can become a development opportunity for their direct reports. For example, while a leader in their division was undergoing chemotherapy, two middle managers told me they were forced to "step up" at work in his absence. One acquired vital coaching skills while working with others in the team on the delivery of a complex project and the other talked about having increased in confidence because of the need to work more autonomously and exercise his own judgment in the absence of his leader.

Despite intense suffering, many individuals see difficult periods in their life as their most powerful learning experiences to date.

Our struggles can become catalysts for professional growth, as it is at times of great pressure that we realize our strengths. If we give individuals adequate time, space and support at work to self-reflect, the culmination of this is heightened self-awareness, which lies at the heart of effective performance. These spaces are critical since the impact of personal trauma on an individual's professional life continues to be poorly understood in organizations.[75] People need to see role models of humility and vulnerability among leaders in their workplace, so that they know it is okay to be open about their own life journeys. Take Jeff Weiner, for example, CEO of LinkedIn, the world's largest professional social network. He has oriented the entire company around compassionate leadership.[76] LinkedIn has grown from 300 employees ten years ago to 12,000 employees today and its enduring culture, which is founded on the principle of trust, differentiates it as an organization. For example, fortnightly all-company meetings are held where Weiner is honest and transparent with all employees about what is happening across the business. The company holds regular 'in days' in which employees are asked to clear their diaries and spend time with their teams. This time away from tasks and targets helps employees to get to know each other better and builds trust and connection.[77] Self-compassion is also encouraged, with each employee being given an annual budget to spend on anything that makes their life easier, such as childcare or a gym membership, and Weiner himself has developed an online course called 'Managing Compassionately'.[78] In this course, he shares his own experiences of the importance of learning to manage with compassion and talks about the need to put oneself in someone else's shoes to try and understand their struggles. He also expresses the importance of team leaders understanding the triggers and vulnerabilities in each of their team members. In an effort to promote and cultivate compassion in organizations across the world, LinkedIn has recently launched a Compassion Award where individuals are invited to submit a 90-second video in which they explain how they are bringing compassion to the world and how LinkedIn might support them. The grand prize winner receives $100,000 to help scale their efforts.[79] On the award's promotional page, the company states:

> At LinkedIn, we believe that leading with compassion is not only a way of making the world a better place, it's a better way of building an organization. We're sponsoring The Compassion Award to foster communication around compassion, to help codify it. The Compassion Award intends to seek out, highlight, and assist leaders who are cultivating compassion in the world.[80]

LinkedIn is a rare example of an organization that is nurturing and promoting compassion; however, compassion is not something that can be mandated. Examples of consciously compassionate companies are starting to emerge in which, like Weiner, their leaders are working to put the systems and practices in place to foster compassion. The next chapter explains what it takes to embed compassion so that it becomes systemic.

7

EMBEDDING
COMPASSION

Many of us have worked in organizations where, for one reason or another, we have suffered in silence. This might be because of insensitive management and our experience of previous disclosures being met with platitudes or lip service regarding our wellbeing. We may also stay silent in the face of relentless work schedules, deciding instead to keep our head down and plug away, rather than admit we are struggling. Perhaps we keep a lid on our angst because we work in a team or department where we do not feel safe to share, or we worry that admissions of vulnerability may be in some way career limiting.

Despite the many work contexts that prevent us from voicing our suffering, spontaneous acts of compassion occur every day. Except by the individuals who are touched by these momentary gestures of kindness, most of these acts go unnoticed. It is more difficult, however, to find evidence of 'consistent compassion', where teams, departments or business units mount a co-ordinated response to individual suffering – in other words, when compassion is organized.[81] There are certain building blocks that enable workplaces to create reliable, consistent and repeated responses to suffering that help to embed compassion.[82] These building blocks are organizational culture, leadership, social networks, and systems and practices.

ORGANIZATIONAL CULTURE

A former CEO of Ford was once reported as saying "culture eats strategy for breakfast",[83] as it is the culture in an organization and its associated norms of behaviour that matter most. Companies can have the brightest visions and the best plans, but if the culture is not conducive, compassion will never flourish. Corporate culture is intangible, but it is felt by all employees. It manifests itself through the stories that are told about the organization both from within it and outside it, as well as its structures, symbols and routines.

Some time ago, I interviewed the CEO of an international bank. Its structure, symbols and routines became evident as soon as I walked into the building. His office was located on the 28th floor, which was only accessible via a private lift. When his personal assistant greeted me, she told me that it was customary for any visitor to the CEO to have a 'meet and greet' from the lift doors so as to make them "feel at home". This experience told me more about the culture of this particular bank than I could have ever gleaned from a 45-minute interview with its boss. For me, the sense of separation between the leader and the bank's employees was palpable. I felt deeply uncomfortable that they rolled out the red carpet just because I was visiting the CEO. It is common in companies for the boss to have their own private parking space, to occupy the biggest office or to be located on the top floor, with the best views, yet each time I experience these symbols of culture I feel there is something unsettling about the CEO being positioned above everyone else in the organization.

In compassionate companies, hierarchy can be difficult to detect. The physical spaces in these companies also look and feel different, such as office layouts, where those in formal positions of power are often being indistinguishable from other employees. Colleagues treat one another with a sense of equality and mutual respect, with no one person being more important than anyone else. When compassion is embedded in culture, the company places its people firmly at its heart. Its values are likely to include words such as 'trust', 'equality', 'balance', 'respect' and 'care', and employees at all levels embody these values in the way they relate to one another as well as the way they interact with their clients or customers.

LEADERSHIP

Whether we like it or not, it is leaders who set the "feeling rules"[84] in an organization, as it is those people who occupy formal positions of power and who set the expectations for what is appropriate when suffering surfaces at work. Compassion is not something that can be mandated from the top down; however, leaders are an inescapable focal point, as they have the power to facilitate compassion and to mobilize resources through the roles they play and the examples they set. When it comes to leadership, stories are important, particularly the stories that leaders tell about their own suffering. Stories can help to build trust, convey values, share a vision of the future and build a sense of collective purpose. It is those leaders who role-model compassion by showing genuine care for others and who have the courage to be honest about their vulnerabilities who build trust quickest. That said, leaders also need to be up to the job. An individual can be the kindest, most caring and most genuine leader in the world, but unless we see them displaying ethical and competent leadership, they tend to elicit pity rather than respect.[85] Equally, those leaders who only project strength and present themselves as the all-controlling, all-knowing hero instead generate fear and mistrust. It is leaders who demonstrate both warmth and competence who create the biggest impact when it comes to creating a culture of compassion.[86]

SOCIAL NETWORKS

Social networks are emotion superhighways at work, since people naturally form webs of relationships where they can gossip, share information, discuss their home life or offer advice to one another. It is the speed and strength of social networks that are the building blocks of corporate compassion.[87] Take the speed of social networks. In the case of an employee's family member being taken ill, for example, how quickly does the news spread within the organization? Is it only the manager who is told, or people within their immediate team, or does news travel across the workforce quickly, so that a collective and co-ordinated response can be marshalled?

At Cisco, an American security and software conglomerate, news of employee suffering travels fast. With over 74,000 employees across the world, one might expect this technology giant's social networks to be slower than those of a small company based on a single site. However, in a 2018 media interview, an employee reported how a leader, whom he had never met, had heard about his daughter's life-limiting genetic condition within the Cisco network and had rallied around her team to raise money for medical treatment, which Cisco then matched.[88] Cisco has become known for its co-ordinated and systemic compassion, which is part of what it calls its 'conscious culture'.[89]

It is not only the speed of connections between people that is important. It is also the strength of social ties that enables compassion to flourish. Managers in organizations that are interested in embedding compassion should be asking themselves, how well do I know each of my team members and how well do they know each other? Do people attend each other's birthday or wedding celebrations? Do they know the names of each other's children? Non-work conversations, time-outs for 'walk and talks', and the availability of communal spaces can help to strengthen the bonds between people. For example, the headquarters of Innocent Drinks in London – the aptly named Fruit Towers building – is designed around communal spaces, with a shared kitchen at its heart. Employees use this space on a daily basis to meet and eat together, and relationships are thereby nurtured and maintained. Strong social ties are founded on trust and mutual respect, which means people are more likely to be aware if one of their colleagues is struggling and more likely to be responsive to them if suffering occurs.

SYSTEMS AND PRACTICES

It is the policies and procedures in organizations that enshrine culture and help to embed compassion. For example, examining the way in which an organization recruits, develops and rewards its people helps to determine the extent to which compassion is both systematic and systemic at that organization. Research has shown that work practices founded upon trust and respect, such as transparent communication, participative decision-making and favourable HR policies, are conducive to a compassionate culture.[90] It is also clear that the companies that promote humanity and dignity throughout their systems and practices experience higher retention and engagement among their staff.[91]

Take the reward practices at Shake Shack, a US fast food chain based in New York. As part of its company ethos to take care of its teams, the food chain is now trialling a four-day working week. In a bid to address low retention levels in the sector, the chain is also using the four-day-week initiative as part of its recruitment drive.[92] In the UK, another fast food chain, Nandos, rewards its employees via a sabbatical scheme. After five years of service, staff are offered a month of additional paid leave. Nandos' employee reward flier reads:

A lot can happen in five years. Even more in four weeks. Congratulations on five PERi-amazing years. There must be something that you've always wanted to do, but never had the time to realize? As our way of saying thank you, we would love to give you an extra four weeks of paid leave to make that ambition a reality. So get out there, have fun and don't forget to let us know what you get up to![93]

Philips, a health technology company, prides itself on its compassionate recruitment process. In addition to taking a traditional approach when interviewing candidates, the company uses an informal style aligned to its values in which people are helped to feel safe and comfortable. I spoke to Aimée, an HR professional at Philips UK, who talked about her experience of being hired. She was asked during the recruitment process to speak about a time when she had been at her most resilient. She decided to talk about the sudden death of her mother, who had tragically died on Aimée's wedding day four years earlier. Aimée said that she had thought twice about making such a personal disclosure so early in her relationship with her potential employer. She felt that it was a big risk, as she had no idea how it would be received, but she felt a strong connection with the company and decided to open up. Aimée told me that the only reason she shared her story was because she felt so comfortable. In her previous organization, where she had worked at the time of her mother's death, she had never disclosed this information so openly. Fast-forward five years and, alongside her current HR role, Aimée now acts as a health and wellbeing champion at Philips. On her web profile, she talks about her personal experience and offers support on issues such as returning to work after maternity leave, meeting the challenges of being a full-time working mum and coping with a sudden bereavement.

Compassionate acts occur in workplaces every day; however, there are building blocks that are required for compassion to become part of an organization's DNA. This chapter has shown that culture, leadership, social networks, and systems and practices must be conducive for compassion to become systemic and flourish.

8

**CONSCIOUSLY
COMPASSIONATE
COMPANIES**

Three very different companies are featured in this chapter, each with a unique story of its journey to becoming consciously compassionate. Yodel is the first case to be presented; it is a parcel delivery business based in the UK with a workforce of over 10,000 people, where compassion hinges on the strength of its social networks. Outpost VFX is presented next. Employing approximately 100 people and producing visual effects for blockbuster films and hit TV shows, this company promulgates compassion through the vision and values of its founder. Finally, a women-only interior design micro-business is featured. Compassion in this company stems from a culture of femininity and friendship.

Before I interviewed leaders from these three companies for this book, they were each sent a list of 12 statements around compassion and asked to assess which of them most closely described their organization. The statements were adapted from research by Monica Worline and Jane Dutton, leading academics in the field of compassion at work.[94] In their book *Awakening Compassion at Work*, Worline and Dutton helpfully include a blueprint for social architecture think about the elements that are required to design for compassion. These are the four building blocks of compassion that were discussed in the previous chapter, and I entitled culture, leadership, social networks and systems and practices. I then used the statements as a basis for my discussions with each company. The 12 statements were as follows:

SOCIAL NETWORKS

1. This organization is characterized by many small clusters of people who know each other well.

2. The quality of relationships in this organization is high.

CULTURE

3. Our corporate values emphasize the importance of people as well as profit or efficiency.

4. This organization strongly values the compassion of its people and its clients.

5. I can easily remember and tell a story of compassion that everyone here would recognize.

LEADERSHIP

6. Our leaders role-model care and concern as a primary part of their work.

7. I can recall several instances when a leader called for compassion in this organization.

SYSTEMS

8. I often hear stories of compassion in this organization.

9. The way that we hire, induct, train, develop and reward includes a significant focus on care for people.

10. People here feel a great sense of responsibility for taking care of others as part of their work.

11. Decisions get made here in ways that reflect great care for people.

12. There is a great deal of autonomy and creativity in the way that people shape their roles here.

YODEL

Yodel is a privately owned distribution business based in the UK. It is geographically dispersed, with over 50 sites across the country, including three main sorting hubs and 47 customer delivery depots, as well as separate office locations for its central support functions such as HR, marketing and finance. Yodel operates at speed and at scale, making over 145 million deliveries to the British public each year. Trailers or parcels arrive into one of the three sortation hubs from Yodel's retail clients, where they are then sorted and distributed to one of its depots before being loaded onto vans for home delivery. The company is headquartered in Hertfordshire and has a workforce of approximately 10,000 people.

A family affair

The last place we might expect to find a consciously compassionate company is in a parcel distribution business. Work in a Yodel depot is neither glamourous nor highly paid. Its warehouse environments are not plush or particularly comfortable, with heavy goods vehicles and vans coming and going. However, despite these basic working conditions, the affection and camaraderie between colleagues are clear. Customer delivery depots are the nucleus of Yodel's social networks, where it is common to have husbands and wives, mothers and sons, and grandparents and grandchildren working together. In many of its locations, it is not uncommon for Yodel to be the main employer in the town, which means that many of its residents rely on the company for their livelihoods. At Yodel, this is something that is encouraged. A flick through the pages of *Our Yodel*, the company's internal newspaper, reveals notices of marriages, profiles of volunteering and fundraising activities, and articles describing how colleagues in the 'Yodel family' have rallied round to support one another. The internal newspaper also promotes the Yodel Foundation, which is a source of financial aid for colleagues and their families during times of hardship. Colleagues are encouraged to fundraise for local charities and for the Yodel Foundation. A recent newsletter stated:

> Many of us go through times that are difficult – whether due to illness, money problems and hardship, or an unexpected turn in life. A financial helping hand can make all the difference and help to turn things around. That's where the Yodel Foundation hardship fund comes in.

Relationships are celebrated in this organization and the depth of the connections between people is evident. This becomes most apparent when something goes wrong. For example, when a van driver was tragically killed by a falling tree during winter storms, his entire depot pulled together to offer their support. The depot manager visited his family and, through the Yodel Foundation, his funeral expenses were covered in full. News of the tragedy spread quickly within Yodel's social network and colleagues from nearby customer delivery depots doubled up on their own workloads so that all of his colleagues could attend the funeral without service delivery being affected. In a conversation with Lynne Graham, Yodel's People Director, she explained to me:

> This sort of thing is really felt in Yodel. It just ripples through the business. Yodel is so much more human than other corporates I've worked in.

At Yodel, the word 'compassion' is not generally used. There is a sense that it is "overly emotional" in this practical, down-to-earth business. Its employees do, however, "look out for one another", with many stories of colleagues coming together in times of hardship. It is when something challenging happens at Yodel that compassion kicks in, and people across the network pull together because they do not want to let their colleagues or customers down. In another instance, a team member had just gone off on maternity leave when her house was burgled and her car stolen. Inside her car had been a new pram and a car seat for her baby. As soon as her team learned of this news, they organized fundraising to pay for replacements. They knew it would not take away the distress of being burgled, but her team wanted to show her that they cared.

This care also extends to Yodel's customers. At busy times of the year, such as Valentine's Day or Mother's Day, Yodel asks for volunteers from all levels across the company to go out and help with deliveries. In one instance, an employee who had volunteered to help out discovered that a bunch of flowers had been sent to the wrong address. To ensure that the customer would not miss out, the volunteer drove 150 miles in her own car to make sure the recipient received her flowers on time.

Compassion in hard times

It is not only when times are financially good that compassion is important for business. At the time of writing, Yodel was in the middle of a financial turnaround and undergoing significant structural and system changes. It could be argued that a consciously compassionate company is only truly tested when it has to handle tough decisions regarding its workforce. In 2017, Yodel made the difficult decision to close five customer delivery depots, knowing that, in certain locations, the closures would be deeply felt in the community. In order to try to make the downsizing process as bearable as possible, the business owners and leaders attempted to ensure their colleagues were treated with dignity and respect. As Lynne recounted:

> This is not just the people who are being made redundant. It's their family and friends who are also impacted. I felt very strongly about that at the time.

In order to support impacted colleagues, Yodel launched an outplacement programme, which included CV writing skills, support with LinkedIn profiles and job interview preparation, and actively contacted other local companies to source alternative job opportunities. Yodel also helped those at risk of redundancy to find alternative work within the company and provided severance packages that went beyond its statutory requirements. All of those who had been affected by the closures were surveyed six months later and were asked how they felt they had been treated during the closure process. Of those who responded, 86% said they had been treated with respect and 78% said they had felt listened to throughout the process. Research on the handling of dismissals and redundancies shows that if it is done compassionately, through sensitive and careful communication, outplacement support and generous severance packages, this can positively influence an employee's perception of the organization after they have left.[95]

Compassion at Yodel is not only directed outwards towards its customers or inwards during times of employee hardship; compassion is also an integral part of leadership development. Leaders and managers across Yodel are encouraged to take care of their own physical and mental health. Yodel's People Director told me that following an innovative leadership development initiative, participants said that they felt more energized and physically active at the end of the programme. The word 'recovery' has become part of everyday language at Yodel, and it is okay to say, "I need some recovery time." This ability to ask for recovery time has been transformational in terms of the way people feel about themselves at work, but without a senior leadership team who allow themselves to be seen and act as human beings, compassion could not have become embedded.

As Lynne shared with me:

> As a leadership team, we are all very accessible. We all bring our own life experiences to the job and are authentic. If you bring your whole self to work with no filter and if you're halfway a decent human being, you'll naturally respond in a compassionate way to situations.

OUTPOST VFX

Outpost is a visual effects (VFX) company that employs around 150 people. It has bases in Bournemouth in the UK and Montréal in Canada, and it has operations in London, Los Angeles and Singapore. Founded in 2012, the company has produced VFX for films such as *Jurassic World: Fallen Kingdom*, *Life*, *Widows* and the Jason Bourne series, as well as popular TV series including *Black Mirror*, *Catherine the Great* and *Watchmen*. After over a decade of working in London and America for some of the biggest companies in the sector, Duncan McWilliam founded Outpost. His vision was to create a VFX studio in a different mould. He shunned a traditional London base in favour of Bournemouth, attracted by its coastal location, and set about pursuing alternative ways of working to offer a new kind of business.

Dreaming of fair trade

When I interviewed Duncan, he told me that he had set about to make Outpost different from other companies in the sector because of his past experience of working for much bigger companies that were profit seeking and shareholder driven, and where people were just numbers. He explained:

> I thought if I could build a company that could retain its staff because it wasn't as driven by profit, or at least there could be flexibility around it, I thought I could retain more staff because they'd be happier, there would be better-quality visual effects and they would keep the knowledge within the company. The idea of a job for life shouldn't be a thing of the past. I would love for it to be something that can be nurtured within a company without [employees] constantly having to jump [to another company] to get a better deal or a nicer environment.

Based in a beautiful, natural environment by the sea and close to a university with good VFX courses, Outpost offers something different from other companies in the sector. Six years after its inception, the company is seeing year-on-year growth in profitability and its workforce is highly engaged – in Duncan's view, because they are happy, well rested and cared for. He explained:

> We've created a structure where we can argue back with our clients and we try and let them understand that we're

a company built around compassion, which is why they should want to work with us. We call it 'fair-trade visual effects'. If you want to buy coffee where you know people are abused in its manufacture, that's up to you. It will probably be cheaper and you can buy more of it. If you want to feel good about what you purchase, you should have the responsibility to do it right and that's where the fair-trade idea comes in. So, if I sell you my company's services and you like that you're spending money with a company that looks after its people, we have more leverage in the market in trying to prevent our people from overwork.

Steve Holmes, Outpost's Head of Marketing, told me that the company's working environment is bright and airy and its physical space facilitates connections between people. There is colour on the walls and music playing in the background, and there are people's dogs in the studio, which gives others a lift when they walk in each morning. The Outpost culture is not just felt via its physical surroundings. The all-company 'Friday Chats' have become a ritual, whereby every week new starters are publicly welcomed, the company says goodbye and good luck to people who are leaving, and news of the vision for the next few months is shared. Instead of just hearing about Outpost's successes, these 'Friday Chats' are also used to talk openly and transparently about things that have not quite gone to plan. Part of Outpost's Friday routine is then to go for 'Friday Beers', where between 30 and 40 employees gather each week at the local pub after work. This ritual is great and, as Steve told me, it is a real "leveller" where colleagues treat one another with a sense of equality and mutual respect, with no one person being more important than anyone else:

> Senior people in the company will sit next to somebody who is 21, and it's their first job out of university, and will talk to them and want to understand who they are. They'll evangelize about what we're trying to do as a company, but also get to know them. And equally you get that with people who've been in the country for five days at that point. They've moved here from Italy, America, Canada, France or Spain and some of them haven't even been to the UK before, let alone this seaside town. And they're sat next to the CEO and everyone else who's been there a long time. And that immediately beds them in a little bit more and makes them feel welcome. You release that pressure valve on a Friday and it levels everyone. Duncan is the first person to go up to a new face and go, "Hi, I'm Duncan," and they might not even know he owns the company.

Upholding company values

It was not long ago that Outpost employed only half a dozen people and was turning over a few hundred thousand pounds. At the time of writing, Outpost's revenue had grown into tens of millions of pounds and the company had just recruited 30 people to its newly opened Montréal base. Growth, however, comes with its own challenges – notably, how to ensure the company's espoused values continue to be reflected in its systems and practices. Duncan had been shocked to read some negative comments on Glassdoor (a website containing anonymous reviews from current and former employees of their place of work) about the long working hours at Outpost. He told me how he had been forced to take a long, hard look at the company to see whether it was delivering on its promise to offer fair trade VFX. At a time when the company was being stretched by the demands of its clients, Outpost's employees were being asked to work longer hours. Duncan found himself in a dilemma. His company had been founded on the principles of fair trade, championing the idea of a workforce who are well looked after and who are protected from being overworked yet, in this period of intense pressure and without a critical mass of employees, people had found themselves working 12-hour days and at the weekends. Duncan said:

> It gave us real pause for thought. We can't just go around saying we're fair trade visual effects, saying we have shorter hours in the contract, but not allowing anyone to make use of it.

Duncan vowed never again to be in a position where he would have to compromise the company's values and, as a direct result of this experience, he decided to offer all employees paid overtime and an unlimited holiday allowance. Life Time, Outpost's uncapped leave scheme, was born. Other companies (such as LinkedIn[96] and Netflix[97]) have been offering unlimited holiday for some time; however, this kind of employee benefit is unprecedented in the VFX industry, where margins are tight and employees are expected to work long, unsociable hours. However, Outpost believes that burnout is the death of creativity, so if their employees are asked to work late, or at weekends, they can now expect to be paid for it and they can also take as much downtime as they need once projects are finished. Duncan explained:

> If we're going to give people flexibility in a very tricky industry, let's give them total flexibility. We trust them to put the extra time in and if we don't repay that trust, then it's just one way. It has to be balanced, which means you've got to be able to take as much time as you need to make sure your life is balanced, so it's not just all about work.

Steve told me that the way holiday requests are approved has also changed. Line managers no longer sign them off in isolation. Instead, they are agreed by consensus in work teams. It is up to individuals, in consultation with their team mates, to discuss when they would like to take time off. Teams self-organize by agreeing to pick up the slack on each other's work while someone is away, and they manage this slack between themselves. As Steve said:

> There's an immediate level of responsibility to those around you, so the scheme doesn't get abused.

Relationships matter

It is the systems and practices in an organization that help to preserve its culture.[98] At Outpost, it is not only its favourable HR leave policies and participative decision-making that enable it to be consciously compassionate; the company also takes a very careful approach to recruitment. Outpost has built an environment in which respectful, warm, kind *and* talented people work together. However, the company has learned from its mistakes, having recruited wrongly in the past and then realized how poor hiring choices are amplified in the behaviours of these people when they join. For example, in one instance a new hire raised their voice at a colleague because something had gone wrong in the studio and in another case team members witnessed a new recruit not treating a fellow team member with respect. Steve explained:

> Those things are very noticeable here. It's like they're glowing in the room when those things happen – you can see them, immediately, and feel it.

As a result, Outpost now consciously works to make sure it gets to know people well before they are hired. This involves many conversations over time with individuals about their passions outside work as well as within, as well as visits to meet staff across the business, so that as many people as possible are involved in recruiting decisions. Once people arrive at Outpost, they are appointed a buddy, who is someone who already knows the company and has been with the business for some time. The company has also recently introduced an initiative whereby anyone can request a non-work chat. This is simply to ensure people have an outlet to talk, should they be facing challenges at home or in their personal lives. It is entirely voluntary, and the individual does not need to chat with someone in a formal position of authority. They can request to talk to anyone within the company, as long as the person has signalled that they are comfortable having these kinds of conversations.

Both Duncan and Steve recounted the same stories of people who had been looked after by the company, regardless of their position, when they faced a difficult episode in their lives. They both recounted the story of a colleague who had had to leave work at short notice to support his father, who had been taken ill. The company supported him to have as much time as he needed with his father and none of the time he took was counted as holiday. Duncan and Steve also both spoke of a colleague who had joined the company just before his wife was due to give birth and therefore did not qualify for statutory paternity leave. He was, however, able to use Life Time, the company's unlimited leave policy, and take two weeks of full paid leave without it counting as holiday. If he needed to take more leave later in the year to be with his wife and baby, he could do so without worrying about his leave entitlement running out. At Outpost, there is no distinction between different levels in the HR policy. As Duncan told me:

It's really important to highlight that if [the person in question is at] the lowest pay grade in the company, that wouldn't make any difference one way or another. Everybody contributes and everybody will be looked after.

As the company continues to grow internationally, Duncan's philosophy is that no one site will expand much beyond 150 people. Compassion is being hardwired into the system because, in his view, among 150 people, the quality of connections can be maintained. As the experience of large companies such as Cisco has shown,[99] it is the strength of many small clusters of people who know each other well and the speed at which news travels across these clusters that enable compassion to flourish. Duncan concluded:

I can't write a compassion policy. It can only be realized and enacted by individuals caring about each other and what they do. I don't want people to care about our brand of Outpost, that's kind of bullshit. You can't care about a limited company registered at Companies House. I would say you can only truly get compassion out of people believing in each other. And that's [accomplished] through small networks.

THE INTERIOR DESIGN PARTNERSHIP

The Interior Design Partnership was formed 15 years ago by four friends: Amanda, Annabelle, Kate, Sarah. They had all held senior roles in industry but, after having given birth to their children, they were looking for a career change. What had once been a hobby and a passion became a business overnight, when they were asked to pitch for the interior design contract for a local show home. After they won the work, their company was born. The Interior Design Partnership is based in Scotland and employs ten women.

Friendship and femininity

This is a women-only company, but this was not by design. When I interviewed one of the leaders, she described how, in the early days, when they were desperate for help, they would ask other mums in the playground if they were interested in part-time work; ten years down the line, the same women now manage part of the business. The company is founded on friendship and has grown organically since. As Amanda told me:

> There's a lot of trust in our business between everybody in the team, a lot of devotion, a lot of loyalty, a lot of respect, a lot of friendship. Friendship is a big thing in the business because that's exactly how the business started.

As the partnership became more successful, the founders realized that their formula worked. They had experienced the hardcore, male-dominated workplaces of the 1980s, where emotions were kept in check. To succeed in business at that time, you could not afford to be feminine as this was considered 'soft'. As Amanda explained, "You couldn't be a woman. You had to pretend to be a bloke." Fortunately, attitudes towards women in business have come a long way since.

The leaders of The Interior Design Partnership believe that the reason their company has survived two recessions and has been successful for so long is because of its culture of friendship and femininity. This translates into a caring and supportive environment in which everyone helps each other to flourish. If someone is irritable and having a bad day, instead of becoming frustrated, the company's mantra is to say, "What can I do to help her?". They describe themselves as a "loving" and "gushy" company. All business correspondence is signed off with a kiss. They give each other hugs and both laughter and tears are regularly shared. Their nurturing approach enables them to get close to their private clients in order to create for them a wonderful family home. As Amanda told me:

> We had a man come to us. A very wealthy man. His wife had left him and taken all their furniture. His house looked like a mausoleum. We entered his life at a time when it was in a mess and he said things like, "I want this to be a wonderful home for my children to come to at the weekend." We did his whole house and we loved doing it, because that's the great thing

about interior design, it can make you feel so much happier if your home feels good. We install the furnishings over two or three days and a customer comes back to a completely transformed house, with all the pictures, mirrors, accessories, everything done beautifully. He couldn't get there when we finished, so we rang him and said, "Can we leave the candles on? How long are you going to be?" He said he was only going to be 20 minutes or something, and we had to go. And he then phoned us in tears when he got home because he was so happy. He said, "You've literally created a family for me. You've created an opportunity for me to have a family in my home."

Within the business, everyone works with a buddy, so that there is a structure of mutual support. This mirrors the partnership between the founders, who all support one another. Furthermore, given that most of the women are juggling work and home pressures, providing flexibility is key. There is a great deal of autonomy in the way people shape their roles in the company, as their lives change over time. For example, some women who joined the company one day a week when their babies were young now work full time managing a team. Decisions get made in ways that reflect care for these women, recognizing that at different life stages, they will have different pressures and priorities when it comes to their work. Instead of losing a good person from the business just because the person cannot see how to make everything fit, the leaders instead encourage the person to craft a role that suits their needs and circumstances. As Amanda explained:

There are people in the office who joke about the fact that they've already resigned four times! We just say to them, "Go away and have a think about it. Have a cup of tea and see if you still feel like that." Or, "Think about what job you would like to do." So, lots of people have evolved their jobs, again, women who have babies, generally, if they can, as their whole emphasis changes [regarding] what's important and how much they want to be at work.

For the founders, there is a commercial reason why they are consciously compassionate. If they are kind to their staff and their staff are kind to each other, they will naturally care for their clients. This leads to better customer service, which generates more referrals. In a situation of business growth, they can then ensure their workforce has the autonomy and flexibility to craft roles that suit them.

Tough love

It has not all been plain sailing. Having navigated their way through two recessions, the founders have had to make tough choices along the way in order to keep the business afloat. These decisions have been particularly painful for them to make, given that friendship lies at the heart of their culture. A pivotal moment for Amanda was learning to come to terms with the duality of being a friend and the boss:

I remember a friend who works for us, who came into work in tears one day. She has three children and they all have problems, so it's constant. I just said to her, "Look, I'm in a really tricky situation here, because as a friend, I want to say, sod work! Go home! Be with your family! But as a business owner, I need you to be here to deliver to the customer. So, let's just have a transparent chat about how it can work for both of us." That was a really defining moment for me.

For the founders, running a consciously compassionate company means being loving and caring, but also being able to have tough conversations when necessary. They talk about the importance of being honest and "levelling with people" if there is a problem that needs to be addressed. Amanda explained that these conversations must be done in a caring way, explaining the reasons why tough decisions need to be made. This is because, ultimately, if the company failed to deliver to its clients, it would struggle to survive. As Amanda explained:

If the leader opens up to the person and gets the elephant in the room out of the way, so to speak, and actually says, "You know what? I'm not the bitch that I might look like when I'm trying to get the work done. I do actually really, really care about you, but I don't know what the solution is here. Because I've got two things going on. One is the caring about you, and in order to care about you, I also have to look after the business. Because I can't care about you otherwise!"

When the company was forced to go through a redundancy process, the founders made sure that they visited those affected at home. This was so that they could explain the reasons behind the decisions that had been taken and break the news to individuals in person, before anyone else in the company was informed. As Amanda said:

> I'm not doing it because I'm horrible to somebody. I'm doing it because it's something we've got to do as a business. I know it's bad news that I'm giving, but I'm not doing it in any less of a loving way.

Given the warmth of their culture, the founders have struggled to come to terms with the formality required around redundancy, such as having to send official letters to those affected. Consequently, each letter always begins with an apology, to explain that the formality is an unfortunate part of the process that they would avoid if they could. The leaders reconcile these tough conversations by keeping the ultimate mission of their business in mind. As Amanda explained:

> I am caring in all of my communication, but still have the goal in mind, which is to ensure that we deliver to our customers. Because ultimately, if we don't, then that affects everybody adversely.

COMMON THREADS

It is possible for compassion to be embedded in any organization – whether it is the size of Yodel, with a workforce of thousands, or a company more like Outpost, with a few hundred employees, or a micro-business like The Interior Design Partnership, employing only a handful of people. The common threads that unite all three of the company case studies featured in this chapter are that in each organization, the leaders are acutely aware of the importance of creating and maintaining a culture that is conducive to compassion. In Yodel, Outpost and The Interior Design Partnership, leaders acknowledge that compassion is only possible if relationships between people across the organization are strong and if that compassion is transmitted through everyone's behaviours. The leaders in these three companies also acknowledge that compassion is not always a bed of roses. In order to preserve the culture and to ensure sustainable business growth, compassion can also sometimes mean having difficult conversations or taking difficult decisions. Consciously compassionate companies ultimately find ways of enshrining their culture by embedding compassion into their systems and practices, so that it becomes hardwired into their processes of recruitment, induction, development and reward so that care for people lies at the heart. As the distinguished professor Raj Sisodia puts it:

> We must pay attention to the 'seed' as well as the 'soil' – the people as well as the organizational context. Even the most extraordinary seed cannot thrive in toxic soil.[100]

9

LESSONS FOR
ORGANIZATIONS

Working people spend as much time with their colleagues as they do with family members; therefore, the way employers respond to employee suffering is crucial. For example, a survey of over 4,000 people found that 56% of those surveyed would consider resigning from their job if they were not treated with compassion following a difficult life experience.[101] Not only is compassion the hidden heart of strategic advantage,[102] encouraging organizations to embed compassion into their systems and practices helps to ensure positive work environments in which individuals are treated with dignity and care. Creating a culture of compassion is an organizational imperative in the 21st century, when suffering continues to be hidden, stress-related absence is growing and career burnout is now a recognized phenomenon.

There are eight key lessons that leaders, managers, HR professionals and colleagues should pay attention to when it comes to fostering compassion at work.

LESSON 1:
START AT THE TOP

Employees who feel loved perform better,[103] but this must start from the top. It is leaders who set the emotional tone in a company, so their behaviours must be congruent with compassion. For example, if they take the time to get to know people regardless of their level, are seen to prioritize employee wellbeing over business outcomes, or are able to show their own vulnerability, this goes a long way in setting a context for compassion to thrive. Given that one in three people are likely to face challenges to their mental health during their working life,[104] leaders must also pave the way by talking openly about their own struggles, as this helps to legitimize the showing and sharing of feelings at work. Take the example of Arianna Huffington, founder and CEO of *The Huffington Post*. Following first-hand experience of burnout, she founded the social movement Thrive Global, which seeks to end the stress and burnout epidemic.[105] Other high-profile executives, such as Geoff McDonald, former Global Vice President at Unilever, have become advocates for the destigmatization of conversations around mental health in the workplace following their own battles with anxiety and depression.[106]

LESSON 2:
LINE MANAGERS ARE PIVOTAL

Behind workload and challenges in our personal lives, management style has been found to be the third most common cause of stress at work,[107] so the way in which line managers respond to employee suffering is crucial. Unfortunately, only one in three of us feel genuinely supported by our organization and less than half of us feel confident in disclosing our suffering to our current manager.[108] Some researchers have suggested that one simple question is required of managers to ensure they bring compassion to their role: *how can I help this person to have a better day?*[109] Line managers should be proactive in their care and concern, but it is important that they ask the individual how they would like to be supported when they are facing a difficult time, and whether they would like their situation to be communicated to other staff or customers. In one instance, for example, a well-intentioned line manager did not inform the rest of the team that one of his direct reports had experienced a child bereavement, believing that he was respecting the person's confidentiality. However, when the individual returned to work, nobody acknowledged the death of his child, so he assumed that everyone was trying to avoid a difficult situation. Finally, it is not just nice to be a nice boss; caring managers and caring colleagues are two of the most important predictors of employee engagement.[110]

LESSON 3:
EVERYONE IS DIFFERENT

It is important to remember that we are all unique. We all have different personalities, life circumstances and ways of coping. During times of personal difficulty, managers should be allowed to be flexible with HR policies to allow individuals to take time away from work, if appropriate, and to choose their own point of return. If they are treated as adults, most people will return to work within a timescale that is seen as acceptable. Managers just need to make sure that they exercise transparency. Every situation is unique, but employees expect fairness, so managers need to be comfortable that any decisions taken to suit an individual's circumstances could be applied again in the same way for someone else.[111] The way in which HR policies are applied has a knock-on effect beyond just the individual concerned and shapes the way all employees view their employer as a result. If an individual is perceived to have been treated unfairly, research has shown that employees question their own commitment to the organization.[112] It should be HR's role to support the line manager in being creative with any policies, rather than being seen as 'the policy police'.

LESSON 4:
WORK IS COPING

For some people, work can be an important distraction when they are facing personal struggles at home. By continuing to work during difficult life experiences, some people find much-needed structure and routine in a life otherwise in disarray. It is especially important to understand that individuals are unlikely to be performing well in these circumstances. When suffering remains hidden, line managers may be unaware that employees are trying to 'work through it' while their life at home is in turmoil. If an employee is not performing well, especially if this continues over a prolonged period, a natural response is to become frustrated and express dissatisfaction. In these situations, managers are better advised to work at suspending judgment and to instead ask questions with care and curiosity,[113] as this may uncover the underlying reasons for a dip in performance. In bereavement situations, particularly, just because there are no physical signs of trauma, it does not mean that the individual is not struggling internally. It may be weeks, months or even years before an individual is able to perform at the levels they once did.

LESSON 5:
BACK TO WORK, NOT BUSINESS AS USUAL

If an employee has taken a leave of absence during a period of personal upheaval, it is important that line managers adjust the person's workload accordingly and remain sensitive to any underlying signs of distress once they return. Line managers should consider the impact of an extended absence on their clients or other team members. This can be an opportunity for work to be delegated and for other members of the team to step up in the colleague's absence or while they are managing a phased return. That said, it is important that this is handled carefully. Managers should be clear about what they expect from those who are taking on the extra work, timescales should be set and the individuals concerned should be rewarded accordingly. Line managers should also consider the impact on those who have stepped up, once the individual is back to full capacity. It can be demotivating for those who have taken on additional responsibility if they are then expected to slot back into their previous role when the individual is back at work. Ideally, line managers should use this as an opportunity to coach team members to find out how new roles or projects might be created to match everyone's strengths and interests.

LESSON 6:
SAY THE RIGHT THING

Well-meaning colleagues can be harmful in their attempts to provide support to an individual who is going through a difficult time, especially when confidential disclosures are met with judgments or trite statements, such as "It can't be as bad as all that" or "You'll get over it." Instead of asking the individual how they would like their situation to be handled, some colleagues just avoid the subject completely, whereas others address their suffering directly when the individual has come to work to temporarily forget. So, what is the right thing to say? Instead of worrying about the 'right' words, colleagues should instead be available to listen without judgment as this has been found to greatly support an individual's healing.[114] Sometimes, individuals just need a sounding board, so colleagues do not have to feel it is their responsibility to solve the individual's problems or offer solutions. Colleagues can become friends and confidantes by just letting individuals know they are there and available should they ever need to talk. At a very basic level, having someone to trust and confide in at work can significantly aid an individual's recovery. Certain dates, birthdays and anniversaries can be very difficult, so for a colleague to acknowledge that they have remembered and are thinking about the person concerned at that time can have a huge impact.

LESSON 7:
GET TRAINED UP

Dealing with employee suffering is a common but complex part of a managerial role, yet management training often lacks the practical content necessary to help managers to hone these skills. For example, line managers, HR professionals and colleagues alike would be well served by learning about the internal processes and external manifestations of grief to understand what an individual may be going through following the death of a loved one. Despite each person grieving in different ways and at different speeds, those working around them may feel better equipped to offer support if they are able to recognize grief's common phases. In the early stages of grief, for example, individuals may be in a state of denial, where they still believe their loved one may walk through the door at any moment. Colleagues of someone in the anger phase of grief may experience their emotional outbursts at work, while the individual processes feelings of frustration. In the later stages of grief, people may seem demotivated, lethargic and depressed.[115] During the grief process, people can behave in ways that are seen as out of character, so it is important not to judge or criticize. When planning learning and development activities, leaders, HR professionals and line managers should consider offering training across a range of topics from handling redundancy to breaking difficult news. When it comes to self-compassion and the importance of spotting signs of exhaustion, for example, some companies are investing in wellbeing training for their executives. Johnson & Johnson, a global medical devices and pharmaceutical company, is one example. It has been reported to have invested $100,000 per person for its senior executives to enrol in its anti-burnout programme.[116]

LESSON 8:
MAKE A SAFE SPACE

Once they are aware of an individual's struggles, it is vital that line managers do not just offer a one-off conversation but continue to create the time and space for confidential non-work conversations. Unless there is a safe environment at work where employees can openly express their emotions without fear of judgment or reprisal, suffering can become "stifled"[117] – that is to say, individuals can become unable to process their feelings and be prevented from healing. If employees have been granted a leave of absence from work, once back, it is important that line managers and colleagues remain sensitive to any underlying signs of distress. Despite appearing to perform on the surface, many people continue to struggle psychologically long after their period of personal hardship. One of the ways in which line managers may learn to pick up on the signs of distress is by getting to know their staff at an intimate level, where details of their home life are shared. This requires a relationship of trust, with trust being built when the manager themselves talks about their own personal life and challenges at home. HR may also consider providing employees with ongoing access to a named member of staff outside the line management relationship with whom they can talk in confidence and through which specialist support can be organized.

CONCLUSION

THE POSITIVE POWER OF COMPASSION IN THE WORKPLACE

These eight lessons are only the start. Each organization has its own context, business priorities, policies and practices that need to be taken into account, which means there is no one-size-fits-all approach when it comes to compassion. However, by fostering genuine care for their people from within, organizations can begin to build healthier professional environments. In their seminal article about the importance of love at work, academics Sigal Barsade and Olivia O'Neill argue that the more love people at work feel, the happier and more engaged they are.[118] (Love in this instance is defined as connection, warmth and affection from colleagues, as opposed to romantic love.) In their research among over 3,000 people in America across seven industry sectors, including financial services, real estate and healthcare, they found that employees who work in a caring culture and who feel safe to express affection and compassion to colleagues report higher levels of job satisfaction and client satisfaction as well as improved teamwork. These employees are also more committed to the organization as a result. Barsade and O'Neill conclude:

> Most importantly, it is the small moments between co-workers – a warm smile, a kind note, a sympathetic ear – day after day, month after month, that help create and maintain a strong culture of companionate love and the employee satisfaction, productivity, and client satisfaction that comes with it.[119]

We may not all be company founders who can create an organizational culture from scratch, by hardwiring compassion into its values and behaviours from day one. We may also not have the formal authority to orchestrate wholesale organizational change to embed compassion within leadership, systems and practices, or social networks. Every single one of us, however, has the power to embed compassion at work. Whether we are self-employed or part of an organization, it is individuals across businesses of all sizes who can embed compassion on a daily basis. It is up to us to become kinder and more compassionate towards ourselves when we suffer, fail or feel inadequate, and we can make choices to demonstrate compassion to others through our actions. So I shall end this book where I began, by encouraging us all to make time for a human moment. It is in these moments that we create opportunities to connect with our colleagues and to build the quality of our relationships at work. When we make time for human moments, we enable people to open up about their struggles and we give ourselves permission to disclose our own. Human moments are important opportunities for us to acknowledge that to be human is to suffer, we are all cut from the same cloth and we are not alone.

ENDNOTES

1. Amy Armstrong, "'I'm a Better Manager': A Biographic Narrative Study of the Impact of Personal Trauma on the Professional Lives of Managers in the UK," (PhD diss., Aston University, 2014).

2. Charlotte Heales, Mary Hodgson and Hannah Rich, "Humanity at Work," *The Young Foundation*, 2017, accessed 10 August 2019, https://youngfoundation.org/wp-content/uploads/2017/04/Humanity-at-Work-online-copy.pdf.

3. Monica Worline and Jane Dutton, *Awakening Compassion at Work: The Quiet Power that Elevates People and Organizations* (Oakland, CA: Berrett Koehler, 2017), 29.

4. Aishah Hussain, "Revealed: The Law Firms with the Best Perks 2018-19," *Legal Cheek*, last modified 4 December 2018, https://www.legalcheek.com/2018/12/revealed-the-law-firms-with-the-best-perks-2018-19.

5. Shiv Malik and Ben Quinn, "Bank of America Intern's Death Puts Banks' Working Culture in Spotlight," *The Guardian*, last modified 21 August 2013, https://www.theguardian.com/money/2013/aug/21/bank-intern-death-working-hours.

6. Jeremy Burke, "Japan is Facing a Death by Overwork Problem: Here's How Companies Are Combatting It," *Business Insider*, last modified 25 March 2018, https://www.businessinsider.com/japan-is-facing-a-death-by-overwork-problem-2018-3?r=US&IR=T.

7. Andy Singer, "The US is the Most Overworked Country in the Developed World: Here's How We'll Change That," *Forbes*, last modified 1 March 2018, https://www.forbes.com/sites/cartoonoftheday/2018/03/01/the-us-is-the-most-overworked-country-in-the-developed-world-heres-how-well-change-that/#15cde5dd1880.

8. "State of the Global Workplace," *Gallup*, 2017, accessed
    10 August 2019, https://www.gallup.com/workplace/238079/state-
    global-workplace-2017.aspx?utm_source=link_wwwv9&utm_
    campaign=item_231668&utm_medium=copy.

9. Dezan Shira and Associates, "How to Manage Statutory Annual
    Leave in China," *China Briefing*, last modified 23 July 2018,
    https://www.china-briefing.com/news/taking-vacations-china-
    understanding-paid-statutory-annual-leave.

10. "State of the Global Workplace," *Gallup*, 2017, accessed
    10 August 2019, https://www.gallup.com/workplace/238079/state-
    global-workplace-2017.aspx?utm_source=link_wwwv9&utm_
    campaign=item_231668&utm_medium=copy.

11. Ibid.

12. Ibid.

13. Zoë Ferguson, "Kinder Communities: The Power of Everyday
    Relationships," Carnegie UK and Joseph Rowntree Foundation,
    2016, 1, accessed 10 August 2019,
    https://www.carnegieuktrust.org.uk/publications/
    kinder-communities-power-everyday-relationships.

14. "All the Lonely People: Loneliness is a Serious Public-Health
    Problem," *The Economist*, last modified 1 September 2018,
    https://www.economist.com/international/2018/09/01/
    loneliness-is-a-serious-public-health-problem.

15. "State of the Global Workplace," *Gallup*, 2017, accessed
    10 August 2019, https://www.gallup.com/workplace/238079/state-
    global-workplace-2017.aspx?utm_source=link_wwwv9&utm_
    campaign=item_231668&utm_medium=copy.

16. Long W. Lam and Dora C. Lau, "Feeling Lonely at Work:
    Investigating the Consequences of Unsatisfactory Workplace
    Relationships," *The International Journal of Human Resource
    Management* 23: 20 November 2012, 4265-4282.

17. "Mental Health at Work Report 2017," *Business in the Community*, 2017, 17, accessed 10 August 2019, https://wellbeing.bitc.org.uk/system/files/research/bitcmental_health_at_work_report-2017.pdf.

18. Zoë Ferguson, "Kinder Communities: The Power of Everyday Relationships," Carnegie UK and Joseph Rowntree Foundation, 2016, 1, accessed 10 August 2019, https://www.carnegieuktrust.org.uk/publications/kinder-communities-power-everyday-relationships.

19. Nick Goodway, "Antonio Horta-Osorio: Insomnia and Me," *The Independent*, last modified 16 December 2011, https://www.independent.co.uk/news/people/profiles/antonio-horta-osorio-insomnia-and-me-6277787.html.

20. Louise Carpenter, "The CEO of Lloyds Bank Turned its Fortunes Around – but the Anxiety Almost Broke Him," *The Times*, last modified 7 October 2017, https://www.thetimes.co.uk/article/the-ceo-of-lloyds-bank-turned-its-fortunes-around-but-the-anxiety-almost-broke-him-fg970cpjr.

21. António Horta-Osório, "It's Time to End the Workplace Taboo around Mental Health" (*The Guardian*), last modified 1 May 2018, https://www.theguardian.com/commentisfree/2018/may/01/removeing-taboo-mental-health-work-lloyds-banking-group-antonio-horta-osorio.

22. See https://www.time-to-change.org.uk.

23. "Mental Health Facts and Statistics," Mind UK, accessed 10 August 2019, https://www.mind.org.uk/information-support/types-of-mental-health-problems/statistics-and-facts-about-mental-health/how-common-are-mental-health-problems/#.XEBxQfn7TIU.

24. "Depression," World Health Organization, accessed 10 August 2019, https://www.who.int/news-room/fact-sheets/detail/depression.

25. FirstCare, "Cost of Absence to UK Economy Rises to £18bn,"
    Personnel Today, last modified 9 March 2017,
    https://www.personneltoday.com/pr/2017/03/
    cost-of-absence-to-uk-economy-rises-to-18-billion.

26. John Fire Lame Deer and Richard Erdoes, Lame Deer,
    Seeker of Visions: The Life of a Sioux Medicine Man
    (New York: Simon & Schuster, 1994), 162.

27. Bronnie Ware, *The Top Five Regrets of the Dying:
    A Life Transformed by the Dearly Departing*
    (London: Balboa Press, 2011), 70.

28. Ann Pace, "Unleashing Positivity in the Workplace,"
    TD Magazine, January 2010, 41-44.

29. Liz Mineo, "Good Genes Are Nice, but Joy is Better,"
    Harvard Gazette, last modified 11 April 2017,
    https://news.harvard.edu/gazette/story/2017/04/over-nearly-80-
    years-harvard-study-has-been-showing-how-to-live-a-healthy-
    and-happy-life.

30. Ibid.

31. Amy Armstrong, Sharon Olivier and Sam Wilkinson, "Shades of
    Grey: An Exploratory Study of Engagement in UK Work Teams,"
    Ashridge Hult, Engage for Success and Oracle, 2018, accessed
    10 August 2019, http://hultmedia.ef-cdn.com/~/media/hultedu/
    executive-education/research/shades%20of%20grey.pdf?la=en.

32. Kristin Neff, "Self-Compassion: An Alternative Conceptualization
    of a Healthy Attitude toward Oneself," *Self and Identity* 2 (2003),
    85-102.

33. Ibid.

34. Kristin Neff and Christopher Germer, "A Pilot Study and
    Randomized Controlled Trial of the Mindful Self-Compassion
    Program," *Journal of Clinical Psychology* 69 (1) (2013), 28-44.

35. Amy Cuddy, Matthew Kohut and John Neffinger, "Connect,
    Then Lead," *Harvard Business Review* (July 2013), 54-61.

36. Jacoba Lilius, Jason Kanov, Jane Dutton, Monica Worline and Sally Maitlis, "Compassion Revealed," *The Oxford Handbook of Positive Organizational Scholarship*, eds. Kim Cameron and Gretchen Spreitzer (Oxford: Oxford University Press, 2012), 273-288.

37. Paul Atkins and Sharon Parker, "Understanding Individual Compassion in Organizations: The Role of Appraisals and Psychological Flexibility," *The Academy of Management Review* 37(4) (2012), 524-526.

38. C. Daniel Batson, "These Things Called Empathy: Eight Related but Distinct Phenomena," in *The Social Neuroscience of Empathy*, eds. Jean Decety and William Ickes (Cambridge, MA: MIT Press, 2011), 3-16.

39. Peter Frost, Jane Dutton, Monica Worline and Annette Wilson, "Narratives of Compassion in Organizations," in *Emotion in Organizations*, ed. Steven Fineman (Thousand Oaks, CA: Sage, 2000), 25-45.

40. Alena Hall, "A Compassionate Work Culture Can Really Benefit the Bottom Line, Too," *Huffington Post*, last modified 29 April 2015, https://faculty.wharton.upenn.edu/wp-content/ uploads/2015/04/A_CompassionateWorkCultureCanReally BenefitTheBottomLine.pdf.

41. Monica Worline and Jane Dutton, *Awakening Compassion at Work: The Quiet Power That Elevates People and Organizations* (Oakland, CA: Berrett Koehler, 2017).

42. Kim Cameron, David Bright and Arran Caza, "Exploring the Relationships between Organizational Virtuousness and Performance," *American Behavioral Scientist* 47(6) (2004), 766-790.

43. Michael West, Regina Eckert, Ben Collins and Rachna Chowla, "Caring to Change: How Compassionate Leadership can Stimulate Innovation in Health Care," *The King's Fund*, 2017, accessed 10 August 2019, https://www.kingsfund.org.uk/sites/default/files/ field/field_publication_file/Caring_to_change_Kings_Fund_ May_2017.pdf.

44. Michael West and Jeremy Dawson, "Employee Engagement and NHS Performance," *The King's Fund*, 2012, accessed 10 August 2019, https://www.kingsfund.org.uk/sites/default/files/employee-engagement-nhs-performance-west-dawson-leadership-review2012-paper.pdf.

45. Kim Cameron, "Strategic Organizational Downsizing: An Extreme Case," *Research in Organizational Behavior* 20 (1998), 185-229.

46. Jody Gittell, Kim Cameron and Sandy Lim, "Relationships, Layoffs, and Organizational Resilience: Airline Industry Responses to September 11," *Journal of Applied Behavioral Science* 42(3) (2006), 300-329.

47. Monica Worline and Jane Dutton, *Awakening Compassion at Work: The Quiet Power that Elevates People and Organizations* (Oakland, CA: Berrett Koehler, 2017).

48. Alec Appelbaum, "The Constant Customer," *Gallup Business Journal*, last modified 17 June 2001, https://news.gallup.com/businessjournal/745/constant-customer.aspx.

49. Ibid.

50. Jennifer Robison, "How The Ritz-Carlton Manages the Mystique," *Gallup Business Journal*, last modified 11 December 2008, https://news.gallup.com/businessjournal/112906/how-ritzcarlton-manages-mystique.aspx.

51. Alec Appelbaum, "The Constant Customer," *Gallup Business Journal*, last modified 17 June 2001, https://news.gallup.com/businessjournal/745/constant-customer.aspx.

52. James Harter, Frank Schmidt and Corey Keyes, "Wellbeing in the Workplace and its Relationship to Business Outcomes: A Review of the Gallup Studies," in *Flourishing: The Positive Person and the Good Life*, eds. Corey Keyes and Jonathan Haidt (Washington, DC: American Psychological Association, 2003), 205-224.

53. Jacoba Lilius, Jason Kanov, Jane Dutton, Monica Worline and Sally Maitlis, "Compassion Revealed," in *The Oxford Handbook of Positive Organizational Scholarship*, eds. Kim Cameron and Gretchen Spreitzer (Oxford: Oxford University Press, 2012), 273-288 at 276.

54. "Lifetime Risk of Cancer," Cancer Research UK, accessed 10 August 2019, https://www.cancerresearchuk.org/ health-professional/cancer-statistics/risk/lifetime-risk.

55. Amy Armstrong, "'I'm a Better Manager': A Biographic Narrative Study of the Impact of Personal Trauma on the Professional Lives of Managers in the UK," (PhD diss., Aston University, 2014).

56. Ibid.

57. All names have been changed for anonymity.

58. Frank Eyetsemitan, "Stifled Grief in the Workplace," *Death Studies* 22(5) (1998), 47.

59. "Mental Health at Work Report 2018: Seizing the Momentum" *Business in the Community,* 2018, accessed 10 August 2019, https://wellbeing.bitc.org.uk/system/files/research/mental_health_ at_work_-_survey_report_2018_-_23oct2018new.pdf.

60. Jason Kanov et al., "Compassion in Organizational Life," *American Behavioral Scientist* 47(6) (2004), 808-827.

61. Jacoba Lilius et al., "The Contours and Consequences of Compassion at Work," *Journal of Organizational Behavior* 29(2) (2008), 193-218.

62. Arlie Hochschild, *The Managed Heart: Commercialization of Human Feeling* (Berkeley: University of California Press, 2012).

63. Mary Ann Hazen, "Grief and the Workplace," *Academy of Management Perspectives* 22(3) (2008), 78-86.

64. John Harvey, Katherine Barnett and Amanda Overstreet, "Trauma, Growth and Other Outcomes Attendant to Loss," *Psychological Inquiry* 15(1) (2004), 26-29.

65. Gianpiero Petriglieri and Sally Maitlis, "Grief is a Universal Human Experience," *Harvard Business Review* (July–August 2019), 116-123.

66. Amy Armstrong, "'I'm a Better Manager': A Biographic Narrative Study of the Impact of Personal Trauma on the Professional Lives of Managers in the UK," (PhD diss., Aston University, 2014).

67. John Van Maanen and Gideon Kunda, "Real Feelings: Emotional Expression and Organizational Culture," *Research in Organizational Behavior* 11 (1989), 43-103.

68. Jane Dutton and Kristina Workman, "Readying for Compassion," paper presented at the Positive Relationships at Work Meeting, Ashland, MA (2012).

69. Ibid.

70. Max Bazerman, *The Power of Noticing: What the Best Leaders See* (New York: Simon & Schuster, 2014), 181.

71. Amy Armstrong, "'I'm a Better Manager': A Biographic Narrative Study of the Impact of Personal Trauma on the Professional Lives of Managers in the UK," (PhD diss., Aston University, 2014).

72. Lawrence Calhoun and Richard Tedeschi, *The Handbook of Posttraumatic Growth: Research and Practice* (Mahwah, NJ: Lawrence Erlbaum, 2006).

73. Amy Armstrong, "'I'm a Better Manager': A Biographic Narrative Study of the Impact of Personal Trauma on the Professional Lives of Managers in the UK," (PhD diss., Aston University, 2014).

74. Jacoba Lilius et al., "The Contours and Consequences of Compassion at Work," *Journal of Organizational Behavior* 29(2) (2008), 193-218.

75. Mary Ann Hazen, "Grief and the Workplace," *Academy of Management Perspectives* 22(3) (2008), 78-86.

76. "Jeff Weiner: Leading with Compassion," Oprah's SuperSoul Conversations, last modified 2 September 2018, https://www.stitcher.com/podcast/own/ oprahs-supersoul-conversations/e/56075237.

77.   Jacob Morgan, "What It's Like to Work at LinkedIn and How Every Company Can Create a Lasting Culture," *The Future Organization*, last modified 7 December 2018, https://thefutureorganization.com/ work-at-linkedin-every-company-lasting-culture.

78.   Jeff Weiner, "Jeff Weiner on Managing Compassionately," In Learning, last modified 31 January 2017, https://www.linkedin.com/learning/jeff-weiner-on-managing-compassionately?trk=li_corpblog_Jeff_Learning.

79.   "The Compassion Award," LinkedIn, accessed 10 August 2019, https://news.linkedin.com/compassionaward.

80.   Ibid.

81.   Jane Dutton, et al., "Explaining Compassion Organizing," *Administrative Science Quarterly* 51(1) (2006), 59-96.

82.   Monica Worline and Jane Dutton, *Awakening Compassion at Work: The Quiet Power That Elevates People and Organizations* (Oakland, CA: Berrett Koehler, 2017).

83.   Dee-Ann Durbin, "Ford Takes Close Look at Itself as Job, Factory Cuts Are Set," *Arizona Daily Star*, 24 January, 2006.

84.   Arlie Hochschild, "Emotion Work, Feeling Rules, and Social Structure," *The American Journal of Sociology* 85(3) (1979), 551-575.

85.   Amy Cuddy, *Presence: Bringing Your Boldest Self to Your Biggest Challenges* (London: Orion, 2016).

86.   Ibid.

87.   Ibid.

88.   Patrick Moorhead, "How Does a 74,000 Person Company Align its Global Leaders in 24 Hours? I asked Cisco Systems," *Forbes*, last modified 1 October 2018, https://www.forbes.com/sites/patrickmoorhead/2018/10/01/how-does-a-74k-person-company-align-its-global-leaders-in-24-hours-i-asked-cisco-systems/#7dab217c7b80.

89. Patrick Moorhead, "How Cisco Fosters a 'Conscious Culture' within the Company," *Forbes*, last modified 19 March 2019, https://www.forbes.com/sites/patrickmoorhead/2019/03/19/how-cisco-fosters-a-conscious-culture-within-the-company/?fbclid=IwAR0zO3E_MwYSjTV3xd8LswR6UqYHURb OsJcpip952YK4mUvGBywgWw_-q8w#66014a6e50b7.

90. Darshna Banker and Kanika Bhal, "Understanding Compassion from Practicing Managers' Perspective: Vicious and Virtuous Forces in Business Organizations," *Global Business Review* 20(6) (2018), 1-17.

91. Patrick Moorhead, "How Cisco Fosters a 'Conscious Culture' within the Company" (*Forbes*), last modified 19 March 2019, https://www.forbes.com/sites/patrickmoorhead/2019/03/19/how-cisco-fosters-a-conscious-culture-within-the-company/?fbclid=IwAR0zO3E_MwYSjTV3xd8LswR6UqYHURb OsJcpip952YK4mUvGBywgWw_-q8w#66014a6e50b7.

92. Nancy Luna, "Shake Shack Tests Four-Day Work Week for Managers," *Nation's Restaurant News*, last modified 18 March 2019, https://www.nrn.com/fast-casual/shake-shack-tests-four-day-workweek-managers.

93. Ella Stephen, post on Nando's UK and Ireland, LinkedIn, page, accessed 30 May 2019, https://www.linkedin.com/company/nando%E2%80%99s-uk-&-ire.

94. Adapted from Monica Worline and Jane Dutton, *Awakening Compassion at Work: The Quiet Power that Elevates People and Organizations* (Oakland, CA: Berrett Koehler, 2017), 199-200.

95. Kim Cameron, "Strategic Organizational Downsizing: An Extreme Case," *Research in Organizational Behavior* 20 (1998), 185-229.

96. Pat Wadors, "Acting Like an Owner When it Comes to Taking Time Off," LinkedIn, last modified 9 October 2015, https://www.linkedin.com/pulse/acting-like-owner-when-comes-taking-time-off-pat-wadors.

97. Daniel H. Pink, "Netflix Lets its Staff Take As Much Holiday as They Want, Whenever They Want – and It Works," *The Telegraph*, last modified 14 August 2010, https://www.telegraph.co.uk/finance/newsbysector/mediatechnologyandtelecoms/7945719/Netflix-lets-its-staff-take-as-much-holiday-as-they-want-whenever-they-want-and-it-works.html.

98. Darshna Banker and Kanika Bhal, "Understanding Compassion from Practicing Managers' Perspective: Vicious and Virtuous Forces in Business Organizations," *Global Business Review* 20(6) (2018), 1-17.

99. Patrick Moorhead, "How Cisco Fosters a 'Conscious Culture' within the Company," *Forbes*, last modified 19 March 2019, https://www.forbes.com/sites/patrickmoorhead/2019/03/19/how-cisco-fosters-a-conscious-culture-within-the-company/?fbclid=IwAR0zO3E_MwYSjTV3xd8LswR6UqYHURbOsJcpip952YK4mUvGBywgWw_-q8w#66014a6e50b7.

100. Raj Sisodia, "Foreword," in *Awakening Compassion at Work: The Quiet Power That Elevates People and Organizations*, Monica Worline and Jane Dutton (Oakland, CA: Berrett Koehler, 2017), ix.

101. "Life after Death: Six Steps to Improve Support in Bereavement," National Council for Palliative Care, 2014, accessed 10 August 2019, http://www.dyingmatters.org/sites/default/files/Life%20After%20Death%20FINAL(1).pdf.

102. Monica Worline and Jane Dutton, *Awakening Compassion at Work: The Quiet Power that Elevates People and Organizations* (Oakland, CA: Berrett Koehler, 2017), 29.

103. Sigal Barsade and Olivia A. O'Neill, "Employees Who Feel Love Perform Better," *Harvard Business Review*, last modified 13 January 2014, https://hbr.org/2014/01/employees-who-feel-love-perform-better.

104. "Employee Outlook: Employee Views on Working Life," CIPD, 2016, accessed 10 August 2019, https://www.cipd.co.uk/Images/employee-outlook_2016-focus-on-mental-health-in-the-workplace_tcm18-10549.pdf.

105. Arianna Huffington, "Burnout is Now Officially a Workplace Crisis," *Thrive Global*, last modified 30 May 2019, https://thriveglobal.com/stories/burnout-officially-a-workplace-crisis-world-health-organization-arianna-huffington.

106. Peter Stanford, "Stress in the City: 'At First I Thought My Depression was a Heart Attack,'" *Daily Telegraph*, last modified 4 January 2017, https://www.telegraph.co.uk/health-fitness/body/stress-city-first-thought-depression-heart-attack.

107. Jill Miller, "Tackling the Top 3 Causes of Stress at Work," *CIPD Community*, last modified 2 November 2016, https://www.cipd.co.uk/Community/blogs/b/jill_miller/posts/tackling-the-top-3-causes-of-stress-at-work.

108. "Employee Outlook: Employee Views on Working Life," *CIPD*, 2016, accessed 10 August 2019, https://www.cipd.co.uk/Images/employee-outlook_2016-focus-on-mental-health-in-the-workplace_tcm18-10549.pdf.

109. Rasmus Hougaard, Jacqueline Carter and Vince Brewerton, "Why Do So Many Managers Forget They're Human Beings?" *Harvard Business Review,* last modified 29 January 2018, https://hbr.org/2018/01/why-do-so-many-managers-forget-theyre-human-beings.

110. "State of the Global Workplace," *Gallup*, 2017, accessed 10 August 2019, https://www.gallup.com/workplace/238079/state-global-workplace-2017.aspx?utm_source=link_wwwv9&utm_campaign=item_231668&utm_medium=copy.

111. Carolyn O'Hara, "How to Manage an Employee Who's Having a Personal Crisis," *Harvard Business Review*, last modified 5 July 2018, https://hbr.org/2018/07/how-to-manage-an-employee-whos-having-a-personal-crisis.

112. Jacoba Lilius et al., "The Contours and Consequences of Compassion at Work," *Journal of Organizational Behavior* 29(2) (2008), 193-218.

113. Emma Seppälä, "Why Compassion is a Better Managerial Tactic than Toughness," Harvard Business Review Online, last modified 7 May 2015, https://hbr.org/2015/05/why-compassion-is-a-better-managerial-tactic-than-toughness.

114. Amy Armstrong, "Six Steps to supporting employees through bereavement," HR Magazine, last modified 17 November 2014, https://www.hrmagazine.co.uk/article-details/six-steps-to-supporting-employees-through-bereavement

115. Elisabeth Kübler-Ross and David Kessler, On Grief and Grieving: Finding the Meaning of Grief through the Five Stages of Loss (London: Simon & Schuster, 2005).

116. Ross Kelly, "New CEO Anti-burnout Program Costs $100,000," Chief Executive, last modified 28 March 2017, https://chiefexecutive.net/new-ceo-anti-burnout-program-costs-100000.

117. Frank Eyetsemitan, "Stifled Grief in the Workplace," Death Studies 22(5) (1998), 469-479.

118. Sigal Barsade and Olivia A. O'Neill, "Employees Who Feel Love Perform Better," Harvard Business Review, last modified 13 January 2014, https://hbr.org/2014/01/employees-who-feel-love-perform-better.

119. Ibid.

ACKNOWLEDGMENTS

It goes without saying that this book would not have been possible without the courage shown by all of the people who have shared their personal stories of suffering. I am grateful and indebted to each one of you. I would also like to thank everyone at Yodel, Outpost and the Interior Design Partnership for giving up their time to share their company journeys in working towards becoming consciously compassionate. These case studies have enabled me to showcase the business case for compassion which is crucial in order to engender change in the workplace. Finally, I would like to thank Colin and Anna who have both been encouraging, curious and patient throughout this process. You are my world and I love you.